Jennifer Du

It's all about connections:
Teachers, Online Communities & PD

Jennifer Duncan-Howell

It's all about connections: Teachers, Online Communities & PD

The use of online communities in the continuing professional development of teachers

VDM Verlag Dr. Müller

Impressum/Imprint (nur für Deutschland/ only for Germany)
Bibliografische Information der Deutschen Nationalbibliothek: Die Deutsche Nationalbibliothek
verzeichnet diese Publikation in der Deutschen Nationalbibliografie; detaillierte bibliografische
Daten sind im Internet über http://dnb.d-nb.de abrufbar.
Alle in diesem Buch genannten Marken und Produktnamen unterliegen warenzeichen-, marken-
oder patentrechtlichem Schutz bzw. sind Warenzeichen oder eingetragene Warenzeichen der
jeweiligen Inhaber. Die Wiedergabe von Marken, Produktnamen, Gebrauchsnamen,
Handelsnamen, Warenbezeichnungen u.s.w. in diesem Werk berechtigt auch ohne besondere
Kennzeichnung nicht zu der Annahme, dass solche Namen im Sinne der Warenzeichen- und
Markenschutzgesetzgebung als frei zu betrachten wären und daher von jedermann benutzt
werden dürften.

Coverbild: www.purestockx.com

Verlag: VDM Verlag Dr. Müller Aktiengesellschaft & Co. KG
Dudweiler Landstr. 99, 66123 Saarbrücken, Deutschland
Telefon +49 681 9100-698, Telefax +49 681 9100-988, Email: info@vdm-verlag.de
Zugl.: Brisbane, Queensland University of Technology, PhD Diss.,2007

Herstellung in Deutschland:
Schaltungsdienst Lange o.H.G., Berlin
Books on Demand GmbH, Norderstedt
Reha GmbH, Saarbrücken
Amazon Distribution GmbH, Leipzig
ISBN: 978-3-639-14081-1

Imprint (only for USA, GB)
Bibliographic information published by the Deutsche Nationalbibliothek: The Deutsche
Nationalbibliothek lists this publication in the Deutsche Nationalbibliografie; detailed
bibliographic data are available in the Internet at http://dnb.d-nb.de.
Any brand names and product names mentioned in this book are subject to trademark, brand or
patent protection and are trademarks or registered trademarks of their respective holders. The
use of brand names, product names, common names, trade names, product descriptions etc.
even without a particular marking in this works is in no way to be construed to mean that such
names may be regarded as unrestricted in respect of trademark and brand protection legislation
and could thus be used by anyone.

Cover image: www.purestockx.com

Publisher:
VDM Verlag Dr. Müller Aktiengesellschaft & Co. KG
Dudweiler Landstr. 99, 66123 Saarbrücken, Germany
Phone +49 681 9100-698, Fax +49 681 9100-988, Email: info@vdm-publishing.com
Brisbane, Queensland University of Technology, PhD Diss.,2007

Printed in the U.S.A.
Printed in the U.K. by (see last page)
ISBN: 978-3-639-14081-1

Contents

Acknowledgements

My gratitude goes to Dr. Margaret Lloyd and Dr. Bruce Burnett for their support and advice throughout this study. A special thanks goes to Dr. Margaret Lloyd for her unwaivering faith, guidance and patience – her constant encouragement has been both an inspiration and lifeline. My thanks and appreciation to Dr Shaun Nykvist for his help and time in creating the online forum.

The study described in this book was made possible by the generosity and support I received from members of the three online communities involved in this study. The sense of enthusiastic support I have received from these communities has been a source of great motivation. I hope that I have been able to give these people a 'voice' and that it is heard clearly.

Finally, I would like to thank my family. Without their patience, humour and understanding this journey would not have been possible.

This book is dedicated to Kaye and Bob Howell. It is also dedicated to all of the teachers who are participating in online communities, may you continue to inspire others to make meaningful use of new and emerging technologies.

Introduction

The impact of the Internet on our lives has been all-encompassing. People are increasingly turning to the social interaction available on the Internet to satisfy their needs, whether these are professional or personal. The Internet offers users fast access to social contacts such as online chat groups and discussion lists helping us to make connections with others. Online communities are being increasingly used by teachers for professional support, guidance and inspiration (Bond, 2004; Cornu, 2004; Matei, 2005). These are often organised around subject areas and offer teachers opportunities to develop both personally and professionally. Online communities are increasingly presenting themselves as a source of continuous professional development for teachers as they are able to deliver authentic and personalised opportunities for learning.

In a career such as teaching, where change is faced continually, whether from new policies, initiatives, developments in pedagogy or the introduction of new technologies, teachers need access to continuous professional learning. But an issue that impacts on this is one of time. Teaching is a profession that does not sit nicely in the traditional 9am-5pm mold. Teachers are often engaged in extra-curricular activities, they have lesson preparation to do, marking and administrative duties to perform. How then do we factor in continuous professional learning? Professional development for teachers has traditionally been offered via after-school workshops, programs conducted on pupil-free days, on the weekend or during school holidays. These all require an effort and attention that may at times be difficult to maintain. Online communities offer another solution. Teachers may access learning at a time suitable to them due to the asynchronous nature of the community, they are able to access a wider, more diverse peer group and they are able to participate as much or as little as their needs dictate. It offers a curious polarity, individualized and personalized learning within a social context. Is it possible that the benefits from both of these distinctly different approaches to learning can be combined and accessed by learners? On the surface, online communities present as the solution to facilitating continuous professional learning for teachers. Or do they?

This book will present the findings of a study that was conducted on three online communities for teachers. Two of these communities were based in Australia whilst the third was a UK-based online community. It will explore the nature of online community membership and examine what types of learning and activities members engage in. It will also seek to determine if such membership has an impact on their pedagogy and look for an answer to the question, is membership a meaningful form of professional development for teachers?

1. Online Communities and Teachers

An online Community of Practice is more than a community of learners

but is a community that learns.

(Schlager, Fusco & Schank, 2002)

The purpose of this book is to investigate online communities of practice as a source of continuous professional development for teachers. Professional development programs "are systematic efforts to bring about change in the classroom practices of teachers, in their attitudes and beliefs, and in the learning outcomes of students" (Guskey, 2002, p.381). Professional development for teachers should provide the basis for continued growth and result in self-sustaining and generative change (Franke, Carpenter, Fennema, & Behrend, 1998) and it has been suggested anecdotally and through small-scale studies (Beames, 2004; Hawkes, 1999; Hunter, 2002; Stuckey, 2004) that online communities have an influential and facilitative role to play in this. The proposition to be investigated is that online communities, due to their availability and the activities and interactions they afford, present as a viable medium for creating genuine opportunities for continued growth and self-sustaining change for teachers.

Background

The impact of the Internet on our lives has been pervasive. People are increasingly turning to the social interaction available on the Internet to satisfy their needs, whether these are professional or personal. The Internet offers users fast access to social contacts such as online chat groups and discussion lists to make connections with others. As Howard Rheingold, a pioneer commentator in this field, observed:

> People in virtual communities use words on screens to exchange pleasantries and argue, engage in intellectual discourse, conduct commerce, exchange knowledge, share emotional support, make plans, brainstorm, gossip, feud, fall in love, find friends and lose them, play games, flirt, create a little high art and a lot if idle talk. People in virtual communities do just about everything people do in real life, but we leave our bodies behind. You can't kiss anybody and nobody can punch you in the nose, but a lot can happen within those boundaries. To the millions who have been drawn into it, the richness and vitality of computer-linked cultures is attractive, even addictive.

> (Rheingold, 2000, p. 4)

What is evident from Rheingold's (2000) description is that richness and vitality are important components to ensure that people continue to actively participate in such a phenomenon.

Virtual communities have their roots firmly in the 1960's Counterculture movement (Goldberger, 2003; Matei, 2005) which advocated authenticity, deeper social involvement, egalitarian ideals, individualism, less prejudice and more emotional satisfaction (Matei, 2005, p. 3). From the general meeting place of people who shared ideas grew subject-specific communities and professional communities.

Online communities are being increasingly used by teachers for professional support, guidance and inspiration (Bond, 2004; Chen & Chen, 2002; Cornu, 2004; Matei, 2005). These have been organised around subject areas and offer teachers opportunities to develop both personally and professionally. The current popularity of online communities means that it is necessary to examine these communities and determine what characteristics are necessary for them to function effectively. It is similarly important to consider the broader impact of participation in these communities on teacher practice.

It is contended that online communities may present as continuous professional development for teachers and that they are able to deliver authentic and personalised opportunities for learning. Professional development for teachers has generally been offered as short courses conducted after school or during school holidays. They have been noted for failing to produce positive results and "traditional forms of professional development are widely criticised as being ineffective in providing teachers with sufficient time, activities, and content necessary for increasing teachers' knowledge and fostering meaningful changes" (Garet, Porter, Desimone, Birman, & Yoon, 2001, p. 920).

Professional development programs are thus seen to be failing to meet the needs of the teachers, students and education policy. As research has shown (Huberman, 1995; Richardson, 1990), there has been little discernible change in teaching practice from current professional development programs, thus an alternative solution is needed. The premise underlying this study is that the use of online communities of practice may present a solution to the failure of current professional development programs in effecting change to teaching practice. Thus it is the intention of this book to investigate if online communities of practice can realise this potential.

Purpose and Aims

The purpose of the study described in this book was to understand how teachers are using their membership of online communities and if these communities can provide meaningful professional development opportunities in return to their members. In particular, it aimed at developing a better understanding of the effect of participation on members' teaching practices and their classrooms.

6

Design of study

The research was conducted within the paradigm of qualitative analysis. The study was conducted as a multiple explanatory case study also known as a collective case study (Yin, 2003). The case to be investigated was the participation and involvement of members in the activities hosted by three online communities of practice. The collective cases, to represent this case, were three online professional communities for teachers – one state, one national and one international. It was not the aim of the study to develop separate detailed case studies of the three online communities involved in the study but to develop a richer conceptualisation of the nature of membership and participation. This approach allowed for a comparative analysis of the results to determine patterns or differences.

The use of a case study approach in this study reflects the current shift in trends of research in education. As Richardson (1994) stated, it has shifted "from a focus on effective behaviours toward the hermeneutic purpose of understanding how teachers make sense of teaching and learning" (p. 5). This shift towards understanding the processes involved in learning is reflected in andragogical learning theories and research in the area of facilitating teacher change. As case studies tend to focus on activities (Creswell, 2005), it was hoped that this approach would provide insight into the learning experiences of the teachers participating in the online communities.

Another trend currently influencing research into education is that "research that gives a voice to practitioners, [which] allows them to communicate their wealth of knowledge to other practitioners and helps them to improve their practice" (Richardson, 1994, p. 5). By seeking the views of members of the selected online communities and analysing their discussions (through the examination of survey responses, transcripts from community discussions and a focus group forum), it was hoped that the case study approach would give the participants "a voice" and that it would be heard clearly. The data for the study was collected through three instruments each drawing directly from teachers' voices. These are:

1   *Electronic survey* - Members of each of the three online communities of practice were invited to complete an electronic (online) survey to determine community demographics, presence of relationships between members and membership characteristics.
2   *Community transcripts* - The online discussion recorded by each of the three online communities of practice through a calendar month (January 2006) was analysed to examine the content of the messages and the impact of membership on teacher practice.
3   *Focus group forum* - Particular members of the three online communities of practice were invited to take part in an online forum to discuss issues which had arisen from the analysis of electronic survey and the community transcripts.

Significance and innovation

The significance of this study lies in its addressing two important areas facing contemporary education. The first is related to the changes wrought to schools and schooling by Information and Communication Technology (ICT) and the need to find meaningful applications of this technology.

Students are exposed to a wide variety of technologies and there is a growing body of teaching professionals able to confidently use it both inside and outside the classroom (Papert, 1993). The availability of the Internet, both at school and at home, has led to an increasing number of teachers accessing information available on the Internet for their learning and for their personal development.

The second area of significance lies in teacher professional development. It has been reported that teachers are largely dissatisfied with the programs currently available to them (Richardson, 1990). Such programs appear to be failing to meet both the needs of the teachers and systemic initiatives (Franke, Carpenter, Fennema & Behrend, 1998). The study described in this book considers both issues and suggests that a solution to the problem of provision of effective professional development for teachers lies in meaningful and applied use of ICT, particularly through Internet-mediated communication tools and the involvement of teachers in online communities of practice.

This is an area where, as previously noted, little research has been undertaken outside of small scale studies (Beames, 2004; Hawkes, 1999; Hunter, 2002; Stuckey, 2004) where the impact on professional development has frequently been an incidental outcome or observation rather than being the purpose of the study. The underlying pedagogical assumption is that knowledge is socially constructed and this study will, significantly, add to the understanding of this assumption in terms of adult and professional learning.

This study involved three online communities - one local Queensland community, one national community and one international community. This has enabled the focus and conclusions reached to be generally applicable to the wider field of the professional development of teachers. The study thus has the potential for informing future professional development programs for teachers and education policy in this area. This potential is in line with current education policy regarding the use of ICT in schools and would make further and better use of the facilities in modern technology-able schools.

In considering the actions (interactions) of teachers in online communities of practice, the observations of Oliver and Omari (1999), in writing of tertiary education, have been realised. They offered that:

> Today, the forms of activity that are frequently suggested as necessary and sufficient conditions for effective university learning are those with high degrees of interactivity and engagement and which provide a motivating environment based on a well structured knowledge base. These activities and conditions incorporate such tasks as the solution of real world problems, students working in collaborative and cooperative teams, problem negotiation and solving, and free and open communication among learners and with their teacher. (p. 58)

Perhaps online communities of practice meet professional development needs because of their involvement in authentic or "real world" problems and in the truly free collaboration wrought by voluntary participation and sharing of experience. This study is significant of its identification of professional development as learning and of the actions (interactions) of online communities as being parallel with students' experiences in online environments. It also places emphasis on the effectiveness of the social construction of knowledge.

The innovation of this study lies in its use of online media in its collection of data. As the subjects for the study were all voluntary members of online communities of practice and dispersed across the world, it was felt that is was both expedient and appropriate to use technological tools (that is, electronic survey and discussion forums) in this way. The community transcripts were similarly drawn from digital archives. This study made technology both the context and content for its investigation.

The analysis of the texts produced through digital media is problematic as it is "a hybrid that is both talking and writing yet isn't completely either one" (Coate, 1997, p. 165). While frameworks exist within the fields of discourse and conversation analysis, these texts require a differing approach. This study, in its investigation of differing modes of analysis and application of both textual and graphic analysis, adds to the knowledge domain of this field.

A further issue of interest to this study, similarly affected by technology, is the problematic definition of "community" in a contemporary context. A traditional or face-to-face community shares some characteristics with an online community but their differences cannot be ignored. The extent of difference can be seen in Woodruff's (1999) abstracted definition of a community as "an amalgamation of ideas" (para. 3). This study has, through the innovative development of a conceptual framework (see Chapter 2), combined the concepts of community, communities of practice, professional development and the learner and therefore attempted to redefine community in terms of the context of this study and in the light of digital communications technologies. This study has added to the knowledge domain of this field through its synthesis of the extant literature into a meaningful conceptual framework.

2. Online Communities, Professional Development and Learning

Members learn both by teaching others and by applying to their own situations the information, tools, know-how and experiences provided by others in the virtual community.

(Hunter, 2002, p.96)

The field of research informing this book are drawn from the field of (a) community, (b) communities of practice, (c) professional development, and (d) the learner. Figure 2.1 shows the interaction of these areas in a simplified conceptual framework with communication (critical to the methodology of the study described in this book) as the central agent binding them together.

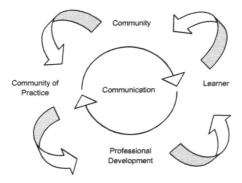

Figure 2.1:   Simplified conceptual framework

Professional development of teachers

Teachers are under constant pressure to learn new skills, update their knowledge and change classroom practices (Richardson, 1990) and as new knowledge or skills are learnt, they need to be absorbed and included in classroom practices. Many researchers perceive teaching to be in a constant state of change as new ideas or developments are disseminated (Borko, Mayfield, Marion, Flexer, & Cumbro, 1997; Gallimore, Dalton, & Tharp, 1986; Richardson, 1990, 1992, 1994, 1997; Richardson & Placier, 2001).

Yet, as noted in Chapter 1, schools have offered teachers traditional workshops conducted after school by an outside expert or by attending conferences during school holidays and it would appear that this has not been as effective as first hoped. Literature claims that short workshops do not encourage the development of new skills nor do they have any long-lasting effect on pedagogy (Boyle, While, & Boyle, 2004; Goldenberg & Gallimore, 1991; Guskey, 2002; Huberman, 2001). Arguably, an alternative mode of delivering professional development which is more complex, long term and embedded in schools (Ingvarson, Meiers, & Beavis, 2003) is needed. The alternative investigated by this book is through voluntary and sustained participation in online professional communities.

Traditional professional development programs appear to be failing to achieve effective change in teachers' practice because the process of how teachers change has been misunderstood (Guskey, 2002, p. 58). In this model, teachers attended workshops, learnt new skills and then went back to their classrooms to use them with their students thus achieving successful change. However, in reality, new skills were not being adopted by teachers nor were they being used in the classroom (Griffin, 1983; Guskey, 2002; Richardson, 1990) since teachers were seeking practical skills that would result in positive change in student learning (Guskey, 2002, p. 59).

Online communities of practice offer teachers a forum to discuss change and gather evidence, mainly anecdotal, of how successful a change was in a classroom. Participants can then decide, based on discussions in chat rooms (Galland, 2002) and through other online media, whether to try the suggested strategies or approaches themselves. This is in direct contrast to the noted unwillingness amongst teachers to use research or implement suggestions by outside experts (Guskey, 1985; 1986; 2002; Richardson, 1992; Richardson & Placier, 2001). Such reported resistance to outside "experts" supports the suggestion that change is an internal process for teachers (Richardson, 1990). Thus the most influential cause of change is personal motivation or perceived need (Borko & Putnam, 1995; Richardson, 1990), rather than external factors such as requirements of the employing organisation or school. Internal factors are not isolated occurrences and would continuously emerge hence reiterating the need for an ongoing or sustained form of professional development. The resistance to outside experts is removed in online communities of practice as change is initiated and supported by peers and the voluntary, rather than forced, participation is the result of internal motivation.

In an attempt to measure the effectiveness of professional development for teachers, Ingvarson, Meiers and Beavis (2003) mapped the relationship between what they described as its background variables (such as individual characteristics and workplace descriptors), structural features (such as contact hours, time span, and participation requirement), the opportunity to learn, the mediating factors and the impact. They also (as shown in Figure 2.2) attempted to map the positioning of the professional community within this relationship showing it as a bridge between individual learning and knowledge.

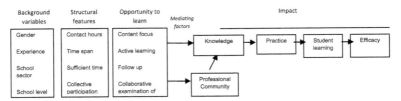

Figure 2.2:   The relationships between structure, learning processes and impact of professional
development programs (Ingvarson, Meiers & Beavis, 2003, p. 29)

An important variable, identified by Ingvarson et al. (2003) as a background variable, is the
individual teacher engaged in the program who will present unique characteristics which need to be
catered to ensure successful engagement in the learning process. Another variable, time, noted as a
structural feature, also needs to be considered. It has been shown elsewhere (see, for example,
Garet et al., 2001) that short professional development programs have been largely unsuccessful
and hence it could be argued that, to develop new skills or affect pedagogy, programs should be
sustained over a longer period of time. Further to this, programs need to allow more time for
teachers to practise what they learn and share their experiences with fellow teachers (Sorge &
Russell, 2000). A clear advantage of online communities of practice (Communities of practice) is that
they, being ongoing and sustained, are not constrained by time limits and members can continue to
participate over a longer period of time.

Consideration also needs to be given to the content of professional development programs.
To ensure that participants successfully engage in the learning process, the content must address
the needs of the teachers, not as more commonly observed, the needs as discerned by school
management or other stakeholders (Sorge & Russell, 2000). Teachers need to be involved in the
planning and implementation of a professional development program to ensure its appropriateness
(Griffin, 1983). The involvement of participants in planning is apparent in online communities of
practice where topics in chat rooms, email lists or discussion boards are usually initiated by
participants and, hence, can be seen to be clearly relevant to participants.

For a professional development program to be sustained, the mode of delivery needs to suit
teacher conditions and be sympathetic to their specific needs as learners. Opinion is, however,
divided on how professional development programs for teachers should be delivered, that is, either
individually or collaboratively. It has, for example, been reported that teacher individualism,
isolation and feelings of self-sufficiency are prevalent within the teacher culture (Hargreaves, 1993),
and that, in order to ameliorate these characteristics, learning for teachers should be conducted
collaboratively (Boyle et al., 2004; Goldenberg & Gallimore, 1991; Greeno, 1998; Hargreaves, 1993;
Huberman, 2001; Kemmis, 1989; Strehle, Whatley, Kurz, & Hausfather, 2001). Collaboration, noted
by Ingvarson et al. (2003) as the structural feature of "collective participation" (Figure 2.2), has been

12

identified as a key practice in online communities of practice and it can be concluded that participation in such a community could meet this identified need of teacher learning.

Collaboration is thus widely identified as an important activity in encouraging teacher learning. Boyle et al. (2004) proposed that collaborative networks are effective as they are often conducted over a longer period of time allowing teachers to learn and reflect on their teaching practices. Networking offers teachers the opportunity to be exposed to new ideas and practices (Huberman, 2001; Strehle, Whatley, Kurz & Hausfather, 2001) and by establishing critical communities of teachers, pedagogy may be improved via a process of critical reflection (Kemmis, 1989). When colleagues are collaborating, they are creating a "narrative of collaboration" (Strehle et al., 2001) derived from shared perspectives that help to create the collective narrative or shared history of the group. This process is dependent upon the communication which was positioned as a central agent in Figure 2.1.

Teacher learning and change

Change is not an isolated period of activity but is continually happening (Richardson, 1992). Gallimore et al. (1986) proposed that teachers are self-regulatory and follow the three stages of Vygotsky's theory of skill acquisition which are (a) external regulation, (b) self-regulation and (c) automatisation in an attempt to meet their needs. What is particular to teachers are the triggers that lead them through these stages which can be caused by stress and disruption to previously acquired skills or by learning new instructional strategies (Gallimore et al., 1986). These triggers continuously appear thus teachers need a resource they can access as they encounter change. This is a role that online communities of practice can assume as their existence is sustained and not limited to a particular session timetabled into teachers work time.

Traditionally, professional development programs aimed at changing teacher behaviour, however, some researchers believe that this is misguided (Borko et al, 1997; Franke et al, 1998; Richardson, 1990) and believe that the focus should be on teachers' practical knowledge and cognition. Teacher change should not be about acquiring a fixed set of skills but in providing a basis for continual growth and problem-solving (Franke et al., 1998). As noted above, the trigger for change is the result of internal motivation; hence, the focus of a program should be on developing cognitive skills that provide a basis for self-sustaining and generative change (Franke et al., 1998).

A widely-held but erroneous belief is that the learning methods used in professional development programs should mirror the methods teachers employ with their students (Terehoff, 2002). This is based on the assumption that children and adults learn in the same way and that pedagogy, the art and science of teaching children is a suitable method to employ when teaching adults. Andragogy, the art and science of teaching adults first proposed by Malcolm Knowles in 1973, is an integrative concept that has been described as a set of guidelines, assumptions or theory about adult learners.

13

Andragogy has been defined as "a set of core adult learning principles that apply to all adult learning situations" (Knowles, Holton, & Swanson, 1998, p. 2) and was based on work by Edward Thorndike (1928), Eduard Lindeman (1926), Cyril Houle (1950) and the field of clinical psychology. These influences are presented in Figure 2.3.

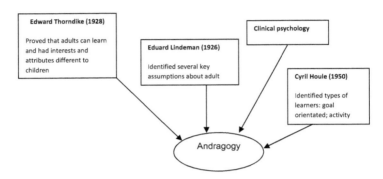

Figure 2.3:   Influences on the development of andragogy

From this background emerged assumptions about adult learners that distinguish them from children. These are: (a) the need to know; (b) the learner's self-concept; (c) the role of the learner's experiences; (d) readiness to learn; (e) orientation to learning; and, (f) motivation (Knowles, 1984). Further to this, adult learners need to know why they are required learn something before undertaking the learning (Knowles et al., 1998) and they have a deep psychological need to be self-directing (Lee, 1998). Adults also have a need to be responsible for their own decisions and, most importantly, need to be perceived by others of being capable of self-direction (Knowles et al., 1998). A distinguishing feature of the adult learner is the wealth of experience they bring with them to the learning environment (Knowles et al., 1998; Lee, 1998) and this pre-knowledge should be treated as a resource and built upon if learning is to be effective. They portray a readiness and orientation to relate their learning to real-life situations (Knowles et al., 1998) or in order to fulfil their role in society (Lee, 1998). Finally, internal motivation is higher than in children (Knowles et al., 1998).

If we accept that adult learners display general characteristics which distinguish them from other types of learners, then andragogy offers a scaffolding to build meaningful learning experiences. When planning an andragogically-based program for teachers, the following guidelines (after Terehoff, 2002) should be considered:

1.   Set up an environment (physical or technological) for adult learning.
2.   Involve teachers in planning the learning program.
3.   Incorporate teachers' needs and interests.

4.   Involve teachers in setting goals and objectives.
5.   Involve teachers in the design of the program.
6.   Involve teachers in the implementation of the program.
7.   Involve teachers in the program evaluation.

A salient feature of adult learning is that it is largely located within the workplace which suggests that the learning will be situated and authentic. For adults, learning is an ongoing and inevitable process arising from participation in work practices across working lives (Billet, 2001b) and a workplace has the potential to enable or inhibit learning. For teachers, a workplace or school culture, composed of interrelated elements (Bean, 2004), has the potential to develop into a community of learners thus affording meaningful professional development for teachers (Shulman & Shulman, 2004).

Defining a community

The study described in this book has taken three online communities of practice as its cases for study. It is therefore of critical importance to investigate what a "community" is and how learning (as professional development) occurs within its formal and informal structures. A community is a phenomenon that is driven rather than something that just happens (Lechner, 1998). Communities, or groups of people, are bound together through some shared connection that transforms a group from individuals to a community. Within the context of education, this binding occurs within online communities of practice formed by teachers with a shared interest in understanding and improving their practice. One of the main concerns for this book is not only defining the notion of community but also unpacking its various components.

An early conceptualisation of community was proposed by Kaufman (1959) who identified it in terms of two polar ideologies. The first described a community characterised by homogeneity, participation and face-to-face contact which reiterates the sense of a bond among members. The second was a cosmopolitan community, characterised by the anonymity and mass contacts which are arguably more indicative of communities that display a shared connection. The most commonly found forms of contemporary online communities would appear to display characteristics of both ideologies, that is, both homogeneous and cosmopolitan, thus suggesting a new or third hybrid grouping containing elements of both. This hybrid form of community could be characterised as homogeneous in purpose, having a dynamic mass membership and being participatory in nature, but lacking the traditional component of face-to-face contact.

A review of the literature defining community reveals a set of complex components which have here been reduced to four, that is, collective, operational, personal and manifest. As shown in Figure 2.4, the current conceptualisation of community can be seen to fall into an emphasis on these four components allowing a clear definition of community to emerge.

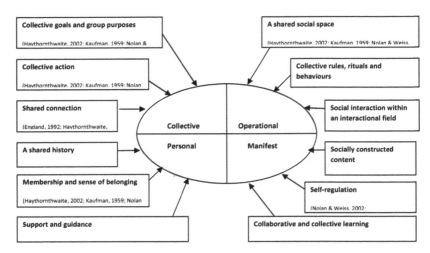

Figure 2.4:   Components of community identified in review of literature

The *operational* components noted in Figure 2.4, that is, a shared social space, collective rules, rituals and behaviours, and social interaction within an interactional field, are primarily concerned with the location and structure of the community. From a social anthropological perspective, a community is made up of people involved in social interaction within a defined geographical area who have more than one common tie (Kaufman, 1959). The interactions of such a community are physically located within what Kaufman (1959) described as the interactional field. In addition, Nolan and Weiss (2002) suggested that a community may also be located in a variety of settings or fields that combine work in real/virtual or online/off-line spaces and that such fields provide the settings for the occasional, periodic or continuous actions (interactions) of that community.

Within the context of the homogeneous collective described by Kaufman (1959), two descriptors have been suggested that describe the shared social space critical for member access and subsequent sense of belonging. Despite the use of two distinct terms - *Interactional field* (Kaufman 1959) and *Common Pool Resource* (Nolan & Weiss 2002) - it would appear that both can be used interchangeably. Embedded within these synonymous descriptors is the social interaction where community activity is based on members communicating and participating. The emphasis on social interaction is deemed to be necessary because "communities are composed of people who live close to each other, who freely share companionship, goods, services and support of all kinds to other members of the community" (Haythornthwaite, 2002, p. 159). What emerges from the literature is the simple but critical notion that a community is reliant upon the shared social space on which it is built.

Implicit within this shared social space are the collective rules, rituals and behaviours which govern social interaction in the community's interactional field. By exploring the way resources are exchanged between individuals and how it creates a connectivity among members of a socially interactive group, such as a community (Haythornthwaite, 2002), a clearer understanding of how the social interaction is maintained emerges. When this perspective is employed, the number and types of resources exchanged and the direction in which they flow helps to clarify the social structure and characteristics of the community which, in turn, helps to identify the type of learning activities the community supports.

The *collective* components noted in Figure 2.4, that is, collective goals and group purposes, collective action and shared connection, are concerned with the community members demonstrating a social collective. A community is a social construct that portrays a shared connection, for example, common goals, values and practices (Riel, 1996), and this may be either a physical connection or a state of being together (England, 1992). This shared connection or bond experienced by members drives the collective action of the group and is the key to transforming a group of like-minded individuals into a community. The emerging community therefore is a group of individuals acting collectively inferring, conversely, that individuals undergo a transformation to fully resolve their membership within the community.

This transformation evolves as a community demonstrates collective goals and group purposes. This has been described as individuation (England, 1992) where individuals take responsibility and develop a sense of autonomy and self-determination within the community they have joined. This, interestingly, is similar to the journey that learners embark on when new members of a community move from peripheral participation towards active full membership (Lave & Wenger, 1991). It would appear that a physical presence in a community does not equate with membership and that the individual must undergo a transformation and develop attributes that enable them to become a participating member of a social collective.

The *personal* components noted in Figure 2.4, that is, a shared history, membership and sense of belonging, and support and guidance, are concerned with how the individual responds to the community and what they receive in return. The understanding of what it is to be a member of a community is dynamic as there are varying levels of participation or involvement but, despite this, what all members are actively creating is a shared history (Haythornthwaite, 2002). This is the result of collaboration and reiterates the role of a shared connection in creating a community and thus ensuring feelings of membership and a sense of belonging which literature has identified as essential in community development (Haythornthwaite, 2002; Kaufman, 1959; Nolan & Weiss, 2002). Community collaboration also provides members with support and guidance (Nolan & Weiss, 2002) which helps to strengthen bonds amongst members.

The *manifest* components noted in Figure 2.4, that is, socially constructed content, self-regulation, and collaborative and collective learning, are concerned with what the community produces. Content is socially constructed by the members within the interactional field. By examining what is referred to as the "curriculum" of the community (Nolan & Weiss, 2002), the nature of the content can be revealed. Three types of curriculum (elaborated in Figure 2.5) were observed in online communities, (a) initiation and governance, (b) access, and (c) membership.

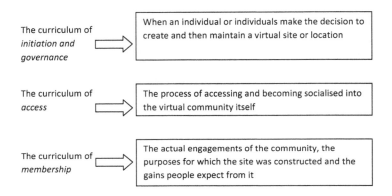

Figure 2.5:   Types of curriculum present in a community (adapted from Nolan & Weiss, 2002)

Examining content via the curriculum structure allows for the isolation and identification of learning objects or experience and implies that community activities are not haphazard or spontaneous but may rather be well thought-out and self-regulating. This may be a guiding influence for the majority of the activities located within the community's interactional field as it is apparent that the activities are driven by the members' collaborative and collective learning strategies.

Summarising the research in the field of communities within the four components, namely, operational, collective, manifest and personal has allowed a simplification and reduction of the many extant definitions and conceptualisations. A further simplified model is presented as Figure 2.6.

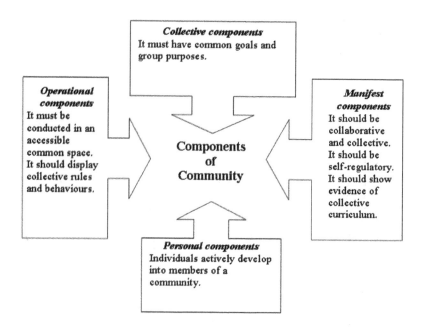

Figure 2.6:   A simplified model of community and its components

From this review of the broad literature on communities, it can be concluded that a community is reliant upon a shared connection between individuals and the interaction of collective, operational, personal and manifest components within the interactional field. The following section will investigate the concept of communities of practice, an extension of communities, and how these communities impact on the professional life of teachers.

Communities of Practice

Communities of practice are people who share a collection of ideas, an activity, or a task. People are eager to find others with whom they share a passionate concern. Still, the value of community is more than affirmation, it involves a search for different ideas, new strategies or practices that might help members re-think their own ways.

(Riel, 1996, p. 5)

In this definition, Riel (1996) implied activity and a sense of connection as distinguishing features of a CoP. Activity is motivated by a need to create new knowledge in order to solve a problem or to

19

expand understanding. When this is applied to teachers, the motivation may be a solution to a pedagogical dilemma, clarification of knowledge or to acquire new content. A teacher's place of work is a large social framework comprised of various departments or grades which can provide a supportive scaffold for workplace learning (Evans & Rainbird, 2002) and, within this environment, differing communities of practice may exist (Wenger, 1998).

The concept of communities of Practice (CoP) arose from the field of situated learning and from the work of Brown, Collins and Duguid (1989). Learning was recognised as being a social phenomenon and Lave and Wenger (1991) viewed learning as the process of becoming a member of what they termed a CoP. To become a fully participating member, the learner moved through stages from being a newcomer to becoming an experienced member. The initial stage was described as "legitimate peripheral participation" which can be seen as being an extension of the idea of a cognitive apprenticeship (Brown et al., 1989). Newcomers develop their knowledge and skills in this space and, as confidence increases and new skills are learnt, they move towards the centre of the community. Lave and Wenger (1991) did not limit participation in communities of practice only to work environments and believed that individuals can be members of any number of communities of practice at any one time.

A CoP is, of course, a group and therefore the dynamics of group learning needs to be briefly explored. Learning can be described as being either surface or deep learning with the latter being promoted through active learner participation (Newman, Webb, & Cochrane, 1995). Learning is an individual process but, in a CoP, it is conducted as a social phenomenon. Learning in a CoP is the result of group activities where members actively participate, to varying degrees, in the creation of knowledge. From this, we can assume that the learning occurring in a CoP is deep learning. Newman, Webb and Cochrane (1995) believed that there is a clear link between critical thinking, social interaction and deep learning.

An individual may be a member of a number of communities of practice at any one time (Lave & Wenger, 1991), but as mentioned previously, must undergo a process or transformation to become a full member. This can be more readily observed in online communities of practice, as newer members tend to sit ("lurk") around the edges of community discussions and contribute significantly less than more experienced members.

As with the definitions of community discussed in previously in this chapter, the notion of communities of practice was developed to describe physical or traditional rather than newer or online communities. The definition of a community of practice has therefore undergone some revision due to the rise of technology-based communities. For example, within the field of situated learning, Putnam and Borko (2000) proposed that interactions with people in their own environment determine what is learned and how the learning takes place and cognition is the result of a system working together. Previously, there would be physical limitations to what could be considered as a person's environment, but as with the online communities of practice examined in this book, physical boundaries are less distinct and what is deemed to be one's "own environment" has changed dramatically. In the past, for teachers, the school would have been the community, but now with Internet access, larger communities are being formed. The physical limitations are removed when participating in online communities of practice and members may come from different schools, states or countries resulting in a richer community and exposure to a variety of perspectives.

It can be concluded that the understanding of what defines a community of practice is changing. What can be agreed upon, and is the understanding to be adopted by this book, is that they are a set of relations among a social collective with a formalised structure, collectively and deliberately embarking on the creation of knowledge. The informal and voluntary nature of membership in a CoP belies the highly structured nature of the community and this has been referred to as the underlying paradox, as a degree of formality is needed to generate a shared repertoire of ideas and resources (Bond, 2004). This formality is apparent when examining the learning activities in Lave and Wenger's (1991) case studies of Yucatan midwives, meat-cutters and Vai and Gola tailors.

An examination of the types of learning activities that occur within communities of practice needs to be considered. The situated approach perceives learning as participation and Lave and Wenger (1991) stated that learning is the process of becoming a full member of a community of practice. This collaborative process, also referred to as collaborative inquiry (Bray, 2002), has been suggested as an effective method for teachers to take responsibility for their learning and thus produce meaningful and enduring results. Collaborative inquiry allows for teachers to receive help, feedback and acquire new skills from their peers and results in an increase in commitment from teachers and a higher likelihood of new practices being adopted (Day, 1999).

At this point, it is useful to consider the two distinct learning perspectives in the field of cognition. The first focuses on the individual's construction and reconstruction of meaning (see, for example, Anderson, Reder, and Simon (1996)) and put simply, is where knowledge is viewed as an entity that is acquired in one context and applied to another. The second perspective focuses on the social collective constructing meaning and attempts to incorporate social and cultural factors into the process of learning. For example, Lave (1988) saw learning as the result of participating in social practice whilst Greeno (1997) perceived cognition as a situated response within an interactive system. From this, and of interest to this study in understanding how learning occurs within communities, is the understanding that learning has two distinct branches - the individual and the social collective. Clearly, the members of a community represent a social collective and the activities they embark on together are an illustration of a social collective constructing meaning together.

Further to this, Hodkinson and Hodkinson (2003) proposed the two rival metaphors of learning to be acquisition and participation. The acquisition learning theory perceives the individual interacting within systems that result in learning (Engestrom, 1999). The participation learning theory perceives the individual subsumed within the social system and learning occurs whilst participating within this system. In either instance, it is clear that learning is, above all else, dependent upon social interaction.

The learning theory, however, which best describes how learning happens in a community is that of situated learning which views activity as central to learning and cognition (Brown, Collins, & Duguid, 1989; Greeno, 1998; Putnam & Borko, 2000). Put simply, knowledge is progressively developed through activity. Brown, Collins and Duguid (1989) proposed that communities of practitioners are connected by socially constructed webs of beliefs which are based upon our conceptual knowledge, which, for teachers, is the result of teacher training courses or from teaching experiences. When teachers are learning how to use this conceptual knowledge, they are like an apprentice who must enter the community and culture to transform these concepts into practical useful knowledge. This transformation must be embedded in authentic situations otherwise knowledge is false (Brown, Collins & Duguid, 1989). An online community of practice, populated with practitioners voluntarily sharing their own practice, is clearly an example of situated learning.

Perhaps one of the distinguishing characteristics that separates a community from a community of practice lies in how a member is perceived. In a community, a member is an equal participant actively involved in the community network. In a community of practice the member is regarded as a learner moving through key stages to become a fully-participating member. The key difference between these two groups is that the motivation for being a member of a CoP would appear to be learning and knowledge acquisition. In a community, membership may be motivated by other triggers such as enjoyment or a shared interest.

The definition of a CoP we have been working towards is, in effect, that of an organisational phenomenon (Bond, 2004) built around generating authentic knowledge. It is a social entity that is recognised as such by its members who are collectively working together in a sense of joint enterprise. Members consciously join a CoP as a result of a desire to learn or extend their knowledge. As Bond (2004), Riel (1996) and Wenger (1998) have independently suggested, a CoP is a group of people who share a passion for something that they know how to do and who interact regularly to learn how to do it better. This joining together of individuals motivated by a group purpose and a desire to create knowledge is the distinguishing characteristic of a CoP that sets them apart from a traditional form of community.

Online communities of practice, also referred to as Internet-mediated communities of practice (IMCoP) (Stuckey, 2004), have the added element of "facilitative" technology, that is, technology that facilitates or encourages communication. For the purposes of this study, the following definition will be used:

> Online communities (for professional development) may be using any form of electronic communication which provides for the opportunity for on-line synchronous/asynchronous two-way communication between an individual and their peers, and to which the individual has some commitment and professional involvement over a period of time.

(Leask & Younie, 2001, p. 225)

An interesting feature of an online CoP is the sense of place it creates in the user as feelings of disconnectedness, isolation and aloneness are reduced. Members do not feel that being in one place cuts them off from other places (Goldberger, 2003). This reinforces the shared connection or bond between members mentioned previously (particularly in the general definition of community) and it has been suggested that the Internet as the facilitative technology being employed encourages the development of this bond (Gray, 2004; Hunter, 2002; Moore & Barab, 2002; Zibit, 2004).

The Internet provides teachers with opportunities to collaborate and reflect with other teachers and experts outside their schools (Hunter, 2002) and makes it possible for individuals to interact, learn and access knowledge and resources within a social space. What distinguishes online CoPs from other online communities is the structure of their learning activities. Wenger (1998) proposed that there are four dimensions of learning within a CoP. These are:

i.   Learning as doing (practice)
ii.   Learning as becoming (identity)
iii.   Learning as experience (meaning)
iv.   Learning as belonging (community)

These four dimensions, consonant with the four components of community presented earlier (see also Figure 2.6), provide a structure for online CoPs to frame their activities around thereby distinguishing themselves from other online communities. Similarity, as shown in Figure 2.7 (an extension of Figure 2.6), can be noted between (a) the practice dimension and the operational component, (b) the identity dimension and the personal component, (c) the meaning dimension and the manifest component, and (d) the community dimension and the collective component.

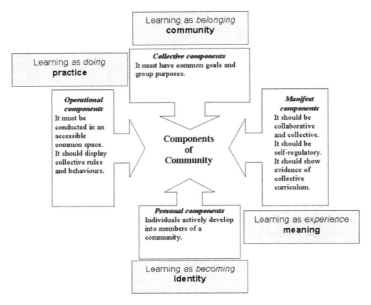

Figure 2.7:   Learning in an online CoP (Wenger, 1998) as an extension of the components of community

Viewing the learning possible within and online CoP as an extension of the previously identified components of community reinforces the concept of a CoP as a highly structured and interconnected environment. It should be noted this environment, positioned within the interactional field, is wholly reliant upon the individual members and their actions as a social collective.

Differentiating between traditional and online community of practice

The reality of being a member of an online CoP, as opposed to a traditional or physical community, is that there is little or no face-to-face social contact with others. As mentioned previously, an online CoP has a formalised structure to organise learning activities around and members of a CoP move through distinct stages of development as they participate in learning (as doing, becoming, experience and belonging) and knowledge acquisition.

An individual in an online CoP is situated in front of a computer terminal and participates through this interface thereby maintaining the locus of knowledge creation with the individual. This is necessary and complementary as knowledge is constructed, as previously discussed in this chapter, individually and collectively, that is, by both social interaction and in the learner's mind (Vrasidas & Zembylas, 2004).

A community of practice moves through several key stages of development (Wenger, 1998) which are characterised by initial periods of intense activity through to a lower intensity in the final stages. This natural attrition is the result of the skill or knowledge having being learnt and absorbed. Once the member of the CoP has reached this point, participation and membership is no longer necessary. However, the nature of online communities of practice may result in a different outcome due to the technology being used, Table 2.1 demonstrates this potential.

Table 2.1

A comparison of the stages of development between a Community of Practice (Wenger, 1998) and an online Community of Practice.

Stages of development	Traditional communities of practice (Wenger, 1998)	As evidenced in online communities of practice
Potential	People face similar situations without the benefit of a shared practice	Potential members familiarise themselves with the learning opportunities the online community may offer and examine the available facilities.
Coalescing	Members come together and recognise their potential	New members familiarise themselves with group activities and tentatively join discussions, whilst learning the norms of the community, this is the process of belonging.
Active	Members engage in developing a practice	Members confidently participate or initiate learning activities.
Dispersed	Members no longer engage very intensely, but the community is still alive as a force and a centre of knowledge	Members regularly participate in learning activities, but may no longer initiate as frequently as previously.
Memorable	The community is no longer central, but people still remember it as a significant part of their identities	Members have the opportunity to return to the community when they need to acquire new knowledge and receive confirmation or support from fellow members. Contact is maintained by regular information sent via email lists.

Online communities of practice are not constrained by time thereby allowing members to move through periods of high to low activity over longer periods of time. The dynamic nature of online membership maintains a freshness and variety that traditional CoP may not be able to achieve. Contact may be maintained between members via group email lists and newsletters allowing members periods of inactivity, yet still maintaining their membership. A distinguishing difference is that online CoP would appear to have the potential to avoid the final stage of development, "Memorable," but instead remain perpetually at "Dispersed" and may be cyclical or continuous as opposed to traditional CoPs which appear to be linear (Wenger,1998). This developmental difference would also affect learning potential, which, in an online CoP learning may be continuous and cyclical whilst in a traditional CoP may be linear and thus limited.

Learning in online CoP occurs primarily through informal interactions among members (Schlager, Fusco, & Schank, 2002) and is a social activity that occurs as new members move through the stages of development and by interacting with experienced members. An online CoP is more than a community of learners but is a community that learns (Schlager, Fusco & Schank, 2002). It is an active learning environment in which learners participate in conversations and inquiry, via chat rooms, email lists and postings ((Leask & Younie, 2001) that authentically establish relevance and meaning (Moore & Barab, 2002).

An interesting cycle, the open collective cycle, was developed by Huberman (1995) which can usefully be seen as a link between professional development and the processes of interaction noted in online communities of practice (see Figure 2.8).

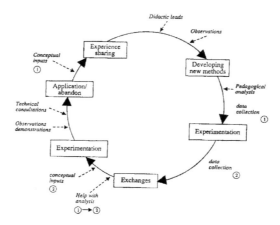

Figure 2.8:   The open collective cycle of professional development (Huberman, 1995).

The open collective cycle of professional development refers to a community that can be developed formally, informally or voluntarily and is a cross section of teachers who share a common interest. It is representative of the cyclical nature of online CoPs and clearly depicts legitimate peripheral participation (Lave & Wenger, 1991) as learners move through stages such as experience sharing, experimentation and application. It clearly shows the stages collaborative communication moves through whilst creating knowledge and could be applied to the learning occurring in online CoP.

Researchers have identified several disadvantages associated with learning in online CoP. The reliance upon text-based communication eliminates physical or visual cues which may result in confusion (Zibit, 2004). Asynchronous forms of communication lack immediacy in exchanges which can prove frustrating (Zibit, 2004) whilst the speed of synchronous communication may not allow time for reading and reflection (Gray, 2004). There may also be technical problems and it has been reported that online communities often fail due to technological gaps and limitations or a lack of appropriate technological infrastructure (Schlager, Fusco & Schank, 2002). Clearly, these are concerns that affect learning which are particular to technology, however there are also potential problems with online CoP conflicting with other communities. Members of an online CoP will also, simultaneously, be members of a workplace-based CoP. As Lave and Wenger (1991) affirmed, there is the potential to be a member of a number of CoPs at any one time. Tensions may develop between the two due to intense involvement in the workplace-based CoP interfering with the participation in the online CoP (Stacey, Smith, & Barty, 2004).

This chapter has attempted to clarify the differences between CoP and online CoP in order to establish the role played by the technology itself in facilitating the actions (interactions) of the community. It has been proposed that the use of technology has changed the stages of development for an online CoP, almost nullifying the final stage. The next section of this chapter will consider the broad area of communication, particularly in online environments.

Communication

As represented in Figure 2.1, the agent of action (interaction) within this study of the role of online communities in the professional development of teachers is communication. It is investigated here in two critical ways. The first is a discussion of computer-mediated communication while the second is concerned with the frameworks being used to analyse online communication.

Computer-mediated communication

Computer-mediated communication has been feted as the facilitator of previously unimagined communicative relationships (Pachler, 2001; Papert, 1993). It can take a variety of forms, with Pachler (2001) offering that:

27

Computer-mediated communication (CMC), be it synchronous, i.e. real-time or asynchronous, i.e. delayed-time, opens up previously unknown opportunities to interact with individuals and groups of people beyond the here and now, and create and share with them social conventions across traditional linguistic and cultural boundaries in so-called virtual communities. (p. 21)

However defining CMC as a mere facilitator of learning limits its applicability, rather than viewing it as a tool for learning, it can be viewed as a new context for learning (Salmon, 2000). An online CoP, being founded in CMC, allows participants to communicate in an environment that encourages discussions beyond physical limitations and provides a new learning domain which enables new and different forms of educational interactions (White, 2003). CMC can be characterised as being open and accessible or as closed and accessible by members only (Pachler, 2001). They are readily available, that is, not hindered by opening hours or other such constraints and offer flexibility not previously available to collaborative learning activities. CMC can be synchronous or asynchronous in nature and Figure 2.9 gives some examples of the type of communicative activities that would be found in either of these groupings.

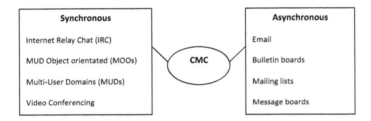

Figure 2.9:   Examples of Computer -mediated Communication (CMC)

Communication occurs largely via the written word in CMC which has given rise to a new written culture (Pachler, 2001) and it is more informal and colloquial in nature. The lack of extra linguistic cues such as facial expressions and gestures has resulted in the use of new linguistic cues such as emoticons and acronyms. These, when combined with expected group behavioural norms, form part of what is collectively called netiquette (Pachler, 2001). These cues have an impact on new users of CMC as they are unfamiliar with those commonly used in the new environment they are participating in, hence, as they move through the process of belonging, they familiarise themselves with them. The use of cues and written communication is not only a communicative tool but helps to create a sense of presence for members.

The discernible presence of the participants, as seen via their written contributions, can be distinguished as being affective, interactive or cohesive responses (White, 2003). Affective responses can be detected via the use of emoticons, humour or self disclosure. Interactive responses can be seen via participation in group activities, such as continuing a discussion thread. Lastly, cohesive responses can be indicative of group commitment such as greeting members by name. The written responses of a member help to create not only a presence in an online CoP but reflect their level of confidence. A disadvantage of written communication is that mistakes are rather public (Salmon, 2000) and this exposure has a marked effect on individuals in the early stages of group membership but as confidence develops, fear of exposure appears to diminish.

Associated with the early stages of group membership and developing confidence are unique behaviours such as lurking or browsing. The levels of participation among members of a community can vary widely but this does not negate or diminish their learning experience and lurking has been perceived as a preferred approach to group apprenticeship (Wild, 1999). New members lurk around the edges of the community learning how to become a member. This process also indicates the lack of traditional hierarchies in CMC, which tend to be dynamic hence the social and contextual cues normally present in group behaviour are missing (Salmon, 2000). Thus it is emerging that CMC offers to be both a tool and unique context for learning.

Literature in this field has identified four advantages associated with this unique context for learning (Pachler, 2001; Salmon, 2000; Wood, 2003). These may be summarised as being:

i.   CMC encourages discussion by facilitating more opportunities for individuals to express their ideas.
ii.   CMC secures fast transmission which allows instant feedback and the ability to save and revisit data.
iii.   CMC allows time for reflection and considered response.
iv.   Written communication results in the participation of all group members equally, for example, active contributors and lurkers.

The unique nature of CMC has given rise to a new form of learning termed "e-learning," which has been defined as both a means of delivering learning outcomes and as a learning experience involving the acquisition or transfer of knowledge through electronic means (Bowles, 2004). It is characterised as being networked (delivered by a computer via the Internet) and catering to individual learner's needs and preferences (Bowles, 2004; Lechner, 1998; Salmon, 2000). Importantly for teachers, it may facilitate lifelong learning, enable workplace learning and encourage collaboration. The transformation from traditional forms of instruction to e-learning is described as being from:

i.   Linear to hypermedia learning
ii.   Instruction to construction and discovery
iii.   Teacher-centred to learner-centred education
iv.   Absorbing material to learning how to navigate and how to learn
v.   School to lifelong learning
vi.   One-size-fits-all to customised learning.

(Lechner, 1998, p. 22)

When learning in online environments, sometimes referred to as e-learning, individuals move through a series of stages; (a) access and motivation, (b) online socialisation, (c) information exchange, and (d) knowledge construction and development (Salmon, 2000). As learners move through these stages, their level of interactivity increases as they move towards more control of the learning experience. This movement through stages is complementary to those of becoming a member of a CoP, they are self-paced, can be asynchronous, allowing members to work in their own time, or synchronous, such as participating in online classrooms, they can be tailored to specific needs and permit more responsibility to be placed in the hands of the learners (Zahner, 2002).

Analysing communication in online communities

How communication in online communities can be analysed is of both theoretical and methodological interest to this study. The use of computer-mediated text messages in research has been well documented (Connelly & Clandinin, 1990; Grabowski, Pusch & Pusch, 1990; Hara, Bonk, Angeli, 2000; Henri, 1992; Levy, 2003) and it is agreed that text-based messages commonly used in computer-mediated communication (CMC) have unique characteristics. Whilst they are written texts, they do not share the same features as traditional written communication (Henri, 1992) and contain more characteristics of spoken communication. It has been suggested, previously, that online or computer-mediated communication is "a hybrid that is both talking and writing yet isn't completely either one" (Coate, 1997, p. 165).

Conversation in online communities is divided into threads with responses to different threads not following logically after one another. This does not inhibit the communicative experience but is merely a distinguishing characteristic of the medium. McCreary (1990) argued that the written word demands an exactness and coherence of thought, indicating that text-based communication results in more well planned and structured interactions. The message itself can be regarded as a complete communicative unit (Henri, 1992) which has its own meaning and structure. A simple framework for analysis (offered by White, 2003) where messages were categorised as being affective, interactive or cohesive was presented in the previous section.

Research has concluded that user participation and motivation increases (Harasim, 1990; McCreary, 1990) when communicating via text-based messages. Harasim (1990) also reported that there is a high level of interactivity in such communication, which, in turn, encourages collaboration and thus influences the learning process. The asynchronous capabilities of text-based CMC allows for more thought, reflection and processing of information (Hara, Bonk & Angeli, 1998).

A widely used framework is content analysis which has been defined (a) as an objective and systematic examination of documents (Babbie, 1990; Kuehn, 1994) and, (b) as a technique aimed at understanding the learning process (Henri, 1992). Content analysis can be used in two ways, that is, to describe a communication phenomenon or to test a hypothesis (Kuehn, 1994). For this study, content analysis will be used to test a hypothesis with discussion transcripts from the three online communities being analysed to determine whether online communities can provide a source of professional development for teachers. This study will adopt the simple definition that content analysis as being a generic name for comparing, contrasting and categorising text (Hara, Bonk, & Angeli, 2000).

Content analysis research on computer-mediated communication has resulted in the development of a number of frameworks for this purpose. For example, Levin, Kim, and Riel (1990) examined interactions found in email messages sent to a group list. The analysis of the topic content of those discussion threads led to the development of *Intermessage Reference Analysis*, which was comprised of graphically representing messages in cluster diagrams and analysing the message act for content.

Similarly, Hiltz (1990) examined the relationship between educational technology and educational effectiveness by sorting data into four categories: technological determinist, social psychological, human relations and interactionist. Other investigations (see, for example, Harasim, 1990) have attempted to establish the existence of knowledge building and examined messages for discernible stages of knowledge building.

One of the widely-adopted content analysis framework CMC was proposed by Henri (1992), who from a cognitive perspective, developed five categories, aimed at revealing the learning process behind the message. These categories were participative, social, interactive, cognitive and metacognitive. This framework for analysis has been used and modified by many researchers. For example, Newman, Webb and Cochrane (1995) used Henri's (1992) five categories but created more detailed sets of paired indicators in an attempt to show evidence of critical thinking and Howell-Richardson and Mellar (1996) combined Henri's (1992) categories with speech act theory to examine the facets of illocutionary acts.

A further extension of the work by Henri (1992) was the *Interaction Analysis Model* (Gunawardena, Lowe, & Anderson, 1997) aimed at contextualising cognitive phases with social interaction and in identifying the strategies used in the co-creation of knowledge. Message were categorised into five phases of interaction, which reflected the movement from lower to higher cognitive phases. This framework was the first to attempt to analyse not just the content of the messages and the learning that was occurring but also incorporated the social construction of the new knowledge being created. It could be proposed that this was the first content analysis method that attempted to incorporate the social aspect of online communities into the analysis of their discussions.

31

From this arose an attempt to understand the structure of the discourses occurring online (Hara et al., 2000). Messages were classified into five categories; elementary classification, in-depth classification, inferencing, judgement and application of strategies. Interactions were mapped electronically to determine the patterns. Similarly, Levy (2003) used a constructivist action-research cycle - planning, taking action, evaluating and theorising - to classify messages in an attempt to understand knowledge construction.

The content analysis framework to be used in this study is the *Practical Inquiry Model* developed by Garrison, Anderson and Archer (2001). This framework was based on and further develops their *Model of Community Inquiry* (Garrison et al., 2001). This earlier model (presented in Figure 2.10) was comprised of three interacting elements, cognitive presence, social presence and teaching presence, which collectively influenced and shaped the educational experience.

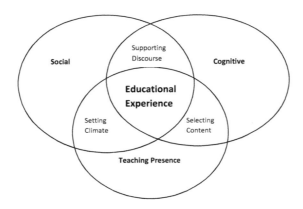

Figure 2.10:   *Model of Community Inquiry (Garrison et al., 2001)*

The *Practical Inquiry Model* (Garrison et al., 2001) recognises and incorporates the shared world and the private world of an individual as important components in the construction of knowledge. This model's strength is its applicability to online Communities of Practice due to the shared/private world perspective. Members participating in online discussion are motivated by experiences in their private world. This framework also represents the social construction of knowledge and the place of the individual within that learning landscape and is therefore consonant with the conceptual framework and the components of community described in this chapter. The Practical Inquiry Model is represented in Figure 2.11.

32

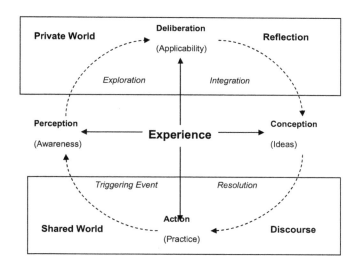

Figure 2.11:   Practical Inquiry Model (Garrison et al., 2001)

The interaction between the shared and private worlds proposed in this model and discussed in detail in the following chapter, can be interpreted as shared, meaning the online community and private, meaning the classrooms of the teachers. The active part of the model, that is, which is the basis of a coding or analysis framework adopted by this study, are the four central phases (triggering event, exploration, integration and resolution). These phases describe a learner's critical thinking process in terms of descriptor codes. While these are discussed in detail in Chapter 3 they are presented in summary as Table 2.2.

Table 2.2

Summary of Phases and Descriptors (based on Garrison et al., 2001)

Phase	Descriptor	Code	Indicators
Triggering	*Evocative*	E1	Recognising the problem
		E2	Sense of puzzlement
Exploration	*Inquisitive*	I1	Divergence – within the online community
		I2	Divergence – within a single message
		I3	Information exchange
		I4	Suggestions for consideration
		I5	Brainstorming

		I6	Leaps to conclusions
Integration	*Tentative*	T1	Convergence – among group members
		T2	Convergence – within a single message
		T3	Connecting ideas, synthesis
		T4	Creating solutions
Resolution	*Committed*	C1	Vicarious application to real world
		C2	Testing solutions
		C3	Defending solutions

Conceptual Framework

The body of research reviewed in this chapter has been synthesised into a conceptual framework (Figure 2.12, introduced as Figure 2.1) which, in turn, was used to inform the findings of this study and guide the methodology. The final version of this framework (Figure 2.12) builds on the previously identified components of a community (Figure 2.4) and attempts to incorporate the characteristics of CoPs as identified by Lave and Wenger (1991). It has also attempted to clarify how an online CoP diverges from a traditional CoP (as noted in Table 2.1) and include these differences, as criteria, within the full framework.

.

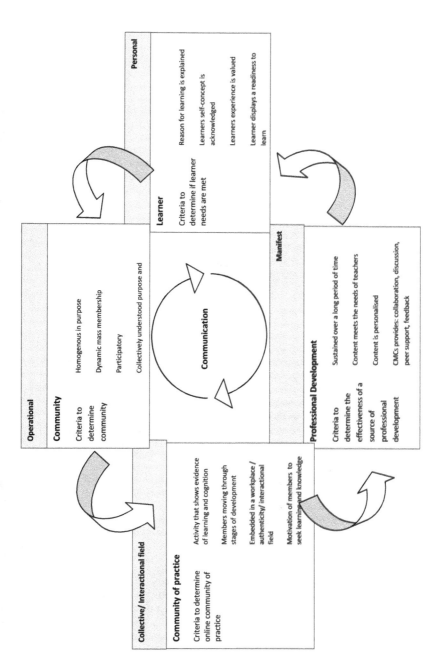

Figure 2.12   Conceptual framework showing identifying criteria and link to components of community

The figure contains the following text:

Operational

Community

Criteria to determine community

Homogenous in purpose

Dynamic mass membership

Participatory

Collectively understood purpose and

Personal

Learner

Criteria to determine if learner needs are met

Reason for learning is explained

Learners self-concept is acknowledged

Learners experience is valued

Learner displays a readiness to learn

Communication

Manifest

Professional Development

Criteria to determine the effectiveness of a source of professional development

Sustained over a long period of time

Content meets the needs of teachers

Content is personalised

OMCs provides: collaboration, discussion, peer support, feedback

Collective/ Interactional field

Community of practice

Criteria to determine online community of practice

Activity that shows evidence of learning and cognition

Members moving through stages of development

Embedded in a workplace / authenticity/ interactional field

Motivation of members to seek learning and knowledge

35

The conceptual framework (Figure 2.12) expands upon the simplified version presented as Figure 2.1 and adds the four components of a community noted in Figure 2.4 (which were also used in Figure 2.7 to explain Wenger's (1998) four learning dimensions). The *operational* components are evident within the criteria to determine community whilst the *collective* components can be found in the criteria to determine an online community of practice. The criteria to determine an online community of practice also acknowledges the importance and presence of the interactional field, a well argued component of a CoP. The *personal* components are evident in the criteria to determine if the needs of the learner are met and lastly, the *manifest* components can be found in the criteria to determine the effectiveness of a source of professional development.

A feature of Figure 2.12 is its listing of criteria for each of the four concepts in the framework. These have been drawn from the literature presented in this chapter (to be detailed in the following text) and serve a critical role in the case study methodology (after Yin, 1994) to be adopted by the study described in this book. The criteria allow the identification of the concept in the phenomenon, that is, the online communities, being studied.

- *Community*

The definition of community reached through an examination of the literature is reliant upon the social interaction between individuals (Kaufman, 1959) occurring within the interactional field. It supports the definition of a group of individuals acting as a social collective (Nolan & Weiss, 2002) collaborating in the creation of knowledge. It was proposed that the understanding of what defines an online CoP was able to support the creation of a third hybrid type of community (Kaufman, 1959) characterised as homogenous in purpose, having a dynamic mass membership and being participatory in nature. It was concluded that a community is distinguished from other groupings by the following criteria:

1.   It has a collectively understood purpose and common goals.
2.   It has a shared social space.
3.   It is collaborative and collective.
4.   Participants display a sense of belonging and membership.

This study assumes that a community is reliant upon social interaction and thus its manifest components are indicative of a social collective constructing meaning together. From the social collective/participatory branch of cognitive learning theory arose situated learning, which viewed activity as central to learning (Brown, Collins & Duguid, 1989; Greeno, 1998; Putnam & Borko, 2000), which when combined with the idea of a social collective learning together in an activity-led participatory approach gave rise to the concept of communities of practice (Lave & Wenger, 1991). This new conceptualisation made the important shift in cognitive focus towards perceiving learning as the process of becoming a full member of a community of practice.

- *Community of Practice*

The second section of the framework is concerned with the criteria to determine an online CoP. The distinguishing feature of a CoP is activity epitomised by an individual moving through an initiation stage towards becoming an experienced member (Lave & Wenger, 1991). As the individual moves through these stages of development, learning and cognition occurs. A CoP is usually embedded within the workplace either physically or technologically, thus making the learning experience authentic (Evans & Rainbird, 2002). A distinguishing feature between a CoP and a more traditional form of community is the motivation of members, as individuals join a CoP for learning and knowledge acquisition.

Online CoP display different characteristics to traditional CoP due to the added element of facilitative technology. The Internet provides a space for CoPs to interact on a much wider scale linking isolated or geographically scattered individuals into a CoP (Hunter, 2002). Initially, a CoP was envisaged as being established within an individual's local environment but the Internet has provided a much wider scope for CoP. Importantly, the stages of development (Wenger, 1998) in an online CoP would appear to be cyclical rather than linear in more traditional CoP. Rather than levels of activity diminishing and eventually expiring, in an online CoP, activity has the potential to maintain itself indefinitely due to the added element of technology which in turn offers more opportunities for sustained learning.

- *Professional development*

The third section of the framework is concerned with the criteria to determine the effectiveness of a source of professional development. CMC has been described as both a tool and context for learning (Salmon, 2000) as it permits flexibility as they are readily available and makes use of a combination of both synchronous and asynchronous programs. In this medium there is reliance upon written communication (Pachler, 2001), which in turn creates a discernible presence of the participants (White, 2003). The use of CMCs has resulted in a new term for the learning activities conducted using this technology, e-learning (Bowles, 2004) and the characteristics and advantages are listed below:

1. CMC encourages discussion by creating more opportunities for expression.
2. CMC permits both instant response and the ability to save and revisit data.
3. Written communication encourages reflection and consideration.
4. E-learning encourages life-long learning.
5. E-learning is learner centred.

(Lechner, 1998, p. 22)

Professional development programs would appear to be failing to meet teachers' needs in their current form (Boyle, While & Boyle, 2004; Guskey, 2002; Huberman, 2001; Goldenberg & Gallimore, 2001). There is a need for them to be sustained over a longer period of time (Ingvarson, Meiers & Beavis, 2003), which can be more easily achieved via the use of ICT. The content of programs should no longer concentrate on teachers' behaviours but focus on the needs of teachers (Sorge & Russell, 2000) which in turn creates more relevancy for participants. Importantly, research has concluded that learning, for teachers, should be conducted collaboratively (Boyle et al., 2004; Goldenberg & Gallimore, 2001; Huberman, 2001; Kemmis, 1989) for example, by creating learning networks similar to online professional communities.

The majority of professional development programs are failing to achieve effective change in teachers (Guskey, 2002; Griffin, 1983; Richardson, 1990). A key requirement for teachers to change is to observe an improvement in their student's learning (Guskey, 2002) which once achieved results in a higher chance of the change being implemented. Teachers are strongly influenced by internal motivation, not the advice of experts (Borko & Putnam, 1995; Richardson, 1990). Change is not an isolated activity but happens continually (Richardson, 1992) and to encourage change in teachers, professional development should not focus on behaviour but on cognition (Franke et al., 1998; Richardson, 1990). Thus professional development programs need to equip teachers with skills that provide a basis for continual growth and development.

ICT has been shown to be a suitable method of delivering and facilitating adult and professional learning. It would appear to encourage learning strategies that have been identified as most desirable for teachers and adult learners such as, collaboration (Hawkes, 1999), group discussion (Merseth & Lacey, 1993), increased dialogue among professionals (Watts & Castle, 1992), peer support and feedback (Merseth & Lacey, 1993; Watts & Castle, 1992). They may be situated within a workplace or at home, providing a higher level of accessibility and thus flexibility in the learning experience (Sorensen & Takle, 2004).

- *Learner*

Adult learners are a homogenous group who display different characteristics and learning requirements from children (Terehoff, 2002). Andragogy, a set of core adult learning principles (Knowles et al., 1998), provides a clearer understanding of the needs and demands of an adult learner. As teachers are adult learners, scaffolding a professional development program upon the six learning principles will help to meet their needs more successfully. The principles are (1) the need to know, (2) the learner's self-concept, (3) the learner's experience, (4) readiness to learn, (5) orientation to learning and (6) motivation (Knowles et al., 1998).

3. Methodology

The extent to which cognitive presence is created and sustained in a community of inquiry is partly dependent upon how communication is restricted or encouraged by the medium.

(Garrison, Anderson & Archer, 2000, p.93)

Online communities are dynamic. At any one time membership numbers fluctuate, who is logged on to the discussion lists will vary or the level of professional expertise may differ greatly amongst participants. These variables will affect the participants' interactions thus requiring a systematic approach to deconstruct these components. Comprehension cannot be achieved by isolating all the variables and examining them separately. Therefore, understanding can only be achieved via an approach that perceives these variables as components of a larger system.

The research study described in this book was qualitative in approach and structured as a collective or multiple explanatory case study (Creswell, 2005; Stake, 1995). As the overarching aim of this study was to investigate online communities of practice as a source of continuous professional development for teachers, the case investigated was the participation and involvement of members in the activities hosted by of three online communities of practice. As previously noted, three communities were selected as the collective cases to represent the general case being studied. These were state, national and international communities to provide a range of professional and geographical environments. This provided a wider scope for the study and ensured a cross-profession perspective. Adopting a collective case study methodology allowed the consideration of experiences, activities, perceptions and outcomes of individuals within the three distinct but similar online communities and permitted an examination of contextual and complex multivariate conditions (Yin, 2003). This methodology also allows the use of multiple data sources and data collection techniques such as archives, interviews, questionnaires and observations (Eisenhardt, 1989) with this study drawing its data from (a) community transcripts, (b) an electronic survey, and (c) an online forum.

Case studies are used to provide insight into an issue (Creswell, 2005) which, as noted for this study, was the potential use of online communities of practice as a source of professional development for teachers. Stake (1978), who perceived case study methodology to be a naturalistic approach to research, noted that "case studies are useful in the study of human affairs because they are down-to-earth and attention-holding" (p. 5). Given its combining of the very "human" process of communication and the practical ("down-to-earth") and self-sustaining ("attention-holding") nature of online professional discussion, any study of online communities is predisposed to case study methodology.

Rationale

The understandings reached in the previous chapter have guided the methodology of this study. The definition of community that informs this study is its being an organisational phenomenon (Bond, 2004) built around the generation of knowledge. This book opened with the statement that an online community of practice is more than a community of learners but is a community that learns (Schlager, Fusco & Schank, 2002, p. 131). This implies that activity is the central tenet in the understanding of community that informs this study. This definition, grounded in understandings of situated learning theories, presumes a community to be a social entity collectively working together (Porter, 2004). A finer working definition was needed, however, to describe where a community of people replaces direct with indirect knowledge of each other and moves their communication into online text-based media. The definition selected was:

> On-line communities (for professional development) may be using any form of electronic communication which provides for the opportunity for on-line synchronous/asynchronous two-way communication between an individual and their peers, and to which the individual has some commitment and professional involvement over a period of time.

> (Leask & Younie, 2001, p. 225)

This definition directs our understanding of community towards three distinct aspects that are present in online communities of practice. The first, the presence of two-way communication, peers to individual and individual to peers. Members can both send and receive messages. Secondly, members of online communities display a commitment of membership to their community and lastly, membership is conducted over a period of time. It is not limited or constrained by time, but is maintained for longer periods.

The conceptual framework (see Figure 2.12) adopted by the study consists of four elements informed by the review of literature. These were (a) Community, (b) Community of Practice, (c) Professional development, and (d) Learner. These form the cornerstones of the methodological approach and will later be seen to be embedded in the propositions and criteria associated with the study's overarching aim.

Case study research

Case studies are a type of ethnography though they differ from this approach in several ways. Ethnography can provide a detailed picture of a culture-sharing group which may be representative or illustrative of a larger process (Creswell, 2005, p. 436). Ethnography can be used to describe and analyse the practices and beliefs of communities (Tesch, 1990). An online community of practice can be considered a culture-sharing group and a detailed examination of them can help to understand their features and limitations. However, a case study description is more concerned with describing the activities of a group rather than reporting on the shared patterns of behaviour, which is more likely to be found in ethnographic research (Creswell, 2005). Case studies are less likely to focus on cultural themes (Creswell, 2005) but rather an in-depth exploration of the case itself. As it was the activities of the online communities, not the shared patterns or cultural themes that the study was most interested in, conducting the study as a collective case study appeared to be the most suitable approach.

Case study research may be conducted either as single or multiple case studies and can be exploratory, descriptive or explanatory (Yin, 2003). Multiple case studies are selected so that they may reiterate each other, in order to provide contrasting or replicated results (Yin, 2003). Multiple case studies also allow for cross-case searches for patterns (Eisenhardt, 1989, p.540). The focus of this study was three online communities, thus it was hoped that this methodology would allow for contrasting or replicated results, or for patterns to emerge clearly.

A case study is an interpretive approach to research. The interpretive perspective perceives intersubjectivity, motive and reason to be central concepts in the approach (Candy, 1989, p. 4). An interpretive approach personalises the research by giving a voice to the participants. By incorporating all of the facets associated with the three elements mentioned above, interpretive research presents a coherent whole (Candy, 1989, p. 5). While there are several extant case study methods, this study has opted to model its method on that proposed by Yin (1994). This method is characterised by its five essential components which are described in the following section.

Case study components

According to Yin (1994), a case study design has five essential components. These are (1) the research question, (2) its propositions, (3) its units of analysis, (4) a determination of how the data is linked to the propositions and (5) the criteria to interpret the findings. These five components, whose interactions are shown in Figure 3.1, will be addressed in the following subsections.

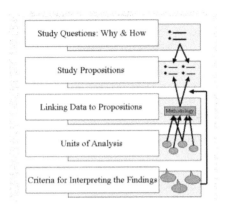

Figure 3.1:   Case study components (Lee, 2003)

Units of analysis

The concept of what constitutes a unit of analysis (a case) in a case study is problematic but at a minimum is accepted to be a phenomenon specific to a time and place (Johansson, 2003). Broadly, the units of analysis (collective cases) investigated were the three online communities involved in the study. Hence, what was being investigated was the participation and involvement of members in the activities hosted by the three online communities of practice.

Determination of how the data will be linked to the propositions

Data was collected through a) community transcripts, (b) an electronic survey, and (c) an online forum. Figure 3.2 demonstrated how the three data instruments were designed to focus on the four elements comprising the conceptual framework. These elements are also shown to be closely related to the aims of the study hence the data is demonstrably linked to the propositions.

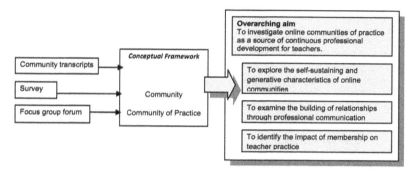

Figure 3.2:   Determining how the data is linked to the propositions

The *community transcripts,* or more properly a collection of discussion transcripts from online communities analysed using the Practical Inquiry Model (Garrison, Anderson & Archer 2001), as a data source were clearly linked to the research question and propositions (aims) and also to the four elements of the conceptual framework. A case study is a naturalistic approach to data collection, as the case under study is an "existing experience" (Stake, 1978, p. 7). Hence it can also be contended that they are outside the realm of control of the researcher. However, data outside of the control of the researcher can be seen as open and unbiased and the use of a multiple case-design is considered to be more compelling and robust (Lee, 2003). The members of the online communities engaged in a range of self-generated discussions on topics of interest or current concern allowing the researcher a glimpse into issues that troubled members. It was interesting to observe that these issues or topics were all able to be categorised under the four elements of the conceptual framework (see Figure 3.2). This reiterated that the areas of concern highlighted by the literature review were the same areas that the members themselves were concerned with.

The *survey* instrument was linked to the research question and propositions and to all four elements of the conceptual framework by virtue of its focus and questions. This instrument was concerned with examining the PD experiences of teachers, their learning experiences online, their opinion of their community and sought to discover if the activities members engage in are indicative of communities of practice. The final data instrument, *the focus group forum* was linked to the research question and propositions and to all four propositions through its eight discussion topics. Hence we can conclude that the data collected was closely linked to the propositions of the study.

Criteria to interpret the findings

The criteria to interpret the findings are the methods of analysis used in the study. This is clearer when these components are viewed as the propositions of the research questions. These propositions guide the criteria to determine the presence of the four components within the online communities involved in the study (see Figure 2.12).

The four elements of the conceptual framework, that is, Community, Community of Practice, Professional development, and Learner, formed the cornerstones of the methodological approach for this study and these elements have been presented in detail as the propositions of the research questions. These are presented in Figure 3.3 (see also Figure 2.12).

Criteria to determine community	*Criteria to determine online community of practice*
• Homogenous in purpose • Dynamic mass membership • Participatory • Collectively understood purpose and goals • Shared social space • Collaborative and collective • Participants display a sense of belonging and membership	• Activity that shows evidence of learning and cognition • Members moving through stages of development • Embedded in a workplace / authenticity/ interactional field • Motivation of members to seek learning and knowledge • Use of technology • The online community shows no evidence of diminishing
Criteria to determine the effectiveness of a source of professional development	*Criteria to determine if learner needs are met*
• Sustained over a long period of time • Content meets the needs of teachers • Content is personalised • CMCs provides: collaboration, discussion, peer support, feedback • Improvement in student learning • Evidence of continuous change in participants professional behaviour • Develops skills for continual growth and development • Accessibility and flexibility	• Reason for learning is explained • Learners self-concept is acknowledged • Learners experience is valued • Learner displays a readiness to learn • Motivation • Learner displays an orientation to learning

Figure 3.3:   Elements of the conceptual framework

Research Design

The research design will comprise an examination of the subjects involved and the sequence of the study. These will be discussed in further detail.

Subjects

The subjects of the study were the members of the three online communities whose participation in their community's activities described the cases (units of analysis) investigated by this study. Each community presents a unique catchment of possible members (see Table 3.1). BECTA Top Teachers is an International community based in the United Kingdom has a membership of 568 whilst Oz-TeacherNet, is a national online community with a broader membership base of 608. The SSABSA – English Teacher community is predominately limited to teachers of English in South Australia and offers a state-perspective to the propositions guiding the research. This community, due to its narrower focus, has a smaller membership of 112. These three communities with their unique membership-catchments provide a comprehensive and wide-ranging scope that permits the conclusions reached in the analysis to have a wider application.

Table 3.1

Overview of online communities involved in the study

Community Name	Organising body	Physical Location	Year founded
BECTA Top Teachers	British Educational Communications Technology Agency	UK	2002
Oz-TeacherNet	Research in Information Technology Education Group	Brisbane (QUT)	1995
SSABSA	English Teachers Senior Assessment Board of South Australia	Adelaide (SSBSA)	2003

Sequence of study

Method and analysis occur simultaneously in case study research (Zucker, 2001). The study was structured around three data collections which occurred across all three online communities. This is shown in Figure 3.3.

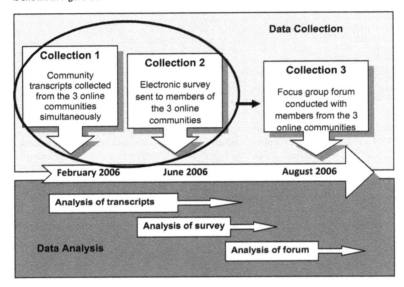

Figure 3.3:   Data collection and analysis sequence

The first two data collections (transcripts and survey) informed the direction of the third collection (forum) which was used to clarify issues or elements that arose. Each of the data collection instruments and analysis informed and directed the following instrument. As the next data instrument was prepared, adjustments could be made to re-focus the data collection on a particular area of concern. Hence the analysis attempted to maintain clarity and integrity by re-visiting the research questions and propositions guiding this study.

Research Method

This section will concern itself with a detailed discussion of the data collection and data analysis conducted in this study. Data collection was via community transcripts, an electronic survey and the transcripts from the focus group forum. Data analysis was conducted on all three instruments, and the details of the tools used to conduct the analysis will be discussed further.

Data Collection

Given that this study has concerned itself with online communities and electronic forms of communication, the data instruments used to collect data reflect this characteristic. The community transcripts (Collection 1) were collected from each online community's electronic archive. An electronic survey instrument (Collection 2) and an online forum (Collection 3) were created and hosted on the Internet.

Community Transcripts

Each of the three online communities involved in the study had electronic archives of transcripts of community discussions. These archives provided rich data for analysis. They were electronic records of email communication between members via the community discussion list. They contained all of the messages members posted to the discussion lists. They have been collected according to calendar months and stored accordingly. Access to the archives was available to members only and required a community username and password. These archives were records for members to freely access to revisit specific discussions, to check their own contributions, to look up information, to catch up with missed discussion and to be directed to by other members. Most list archives are searchable by author and subject as well as date of posting.

It was decided that to simplify the data collection, the transcripts for the same month would be collected for each online community. After examination of the file size per month, it was determined that certain months had larger file sizes. In order to have access to rich data, it was decided that a large file size month would be selected. The three online communities represented three unique contexts; a state community (SSABSA), a national community (OzTeacherNet) and an international community (BECTA). Two of the communities, SSABSA and OzTeacherNet were Australian-based and it could be assumed followed similar patterns of high and low activity due to similar school calendars. It was decided that January continued to present as a very active month, due to the file sizes in the archive. This was also true in the international community, BECTA. Thus the month of January was selected. This presented the context of two communities preparing for the new school year and one community half-way through their academic year. The community transcripts were downloaded and stored electronically. These were then loaded into the qualitative analysis program, MAXqda2® for coding and analysis.

Survey

The electronic survey was created with the assistance of a University technician and comprised of a combination of 25 open and closed questions (See Appendix 1). It was organised around four topics (a) background (b) professional development, (c) online communities, and (d) ICT use. These topics emerged as areas of interest from the literature review. It was hoped that data would be collected that would support the conclusions reached in literature review and the propositions suggested in the conceptual framework (see Figure 2.8).

As mentioned above, the questions in each section were carefully constructed to support the propositions suggested in the conceptual framework and in keeping with the initial conclusions reached in chapter 2. For section (a) background, the questions aimed at collecting broad demographic data and answered the who/ what/ why/ how continuum. Section (b) professional development sought to explore the professional development experiences of members and elicit personal opinions and suggestions regarding this topic. Section (c) online communities was designed to clarify the nature of the respondents membership to the online community and their motivation for joining. Finally, section (d) ICT skills sought to ascertain how members obtained their ICT skills. The questions were constructed in keeping with these aims and were guided by the literature review.

The electronic survey was hosted by the University server for a period of three weeks. The members of the three online communities were invited to complete the survey via a request posted to the community email list. The email message contained a link to the survey. Firstly the respondent was asked to read an information document outlining the research project and how the data collected was to be used. As mentioned previously, the survey was available for three weeks and members were sent a 'reminder' email encouraging them to participate after the first two weeks had elapsed. The survey had a consent mechanism built into the first page where respondents recorded their consent to participate in the research by selecting the 'Start Survey' button. All responses were anonymous and no personal details such as email or IP addresses were collected thereby ensuring privacy. This meant that the respondents could not be identified.

The results of the survey were collected in an *Excel®* spreadsheet format. This raw data was then tabulated and sorted for analysis. The survey was available from the second week of May 2006 and closed during the first week of June 2006.

Forum

The focus group forum was the final data instrument used in the study. As demonstrated by Figure 3.3, the initial analysis of the transcripts and survey informed the direction of the forum. This instrument was created in order to clarify and elucidate elements that emerged from the survey and transcripts. Participants in the focus group forum were recruited via convenience sampling. Convenience sampling (Stewart & Shamdasani, 1990) is one of the most popular forms of recruiting for focus groups as it saves the researcher time and in some cases money. As Stewart and Shamdasani (1990) noted "the intent of virtually all focus groups is to draw some conclusions about a population of interest, so the group must consist of representative members of the larger population" (p.53).

The focus group comprised of members of the three online communities involved in the study. An informal survey was conducted to determine the most active members of each community over a three month period. These identified members were sent an inviting them to participate in the forum. Members were asked to complete an electronic permission form and 2 to 3 members were invited from each community. Whilst the aim was for optimally 9 participants, in order to avoid 'no shows' more were invited.

Online forums have a number of advantages as they provide a facility to "develop ideas and questions but also to store these ideas and questions so that they are always available for further discussion and revision" (Li, 2004, p.24). The questions used to start the forum were framed from the discrete areas of interest arising from the survey and community transcripts (Table 3.2). The questions were organised into subject areas to avoid confusions (Li, 2004, p. 27). The forum was available to participants for 3 weeks in August 2006 and a reminder email was sent to participants after the initial week of activity. The researcher participated in the forum discussions by posting the initial question and sending messages prompting members for further clarification.

As it has been previously noted, the initial analysis of the transcripts and survey informed the questions that were constructed for the forum. This was purposeful and aimed at clarifying and elucidating elements or themes that had emerged from the initial analysis. The eight broad subject areas were selected as they had emerged as areas of focus from the literature review and reflected the aims of the project. The questions were directly in response to issues that needed clarifying after the initial analysis of the survey and transcripts.

The forum was divided into eight electronic pages, with the subject area displayed as the topic and the question posted to start the discussion. These questions can be seen in Table 3.2. At the end of three weeks, the data was collected into eight separate electronic documents.

Table 3.2

Subject area and questions from the forum

Subject area	Question to start the discussion
Impact on classroom	Have you used any ideas from community discussions or activities in your classroom?
Relationships	Have you formed closer personal relationships with any members? For example, are there any members you met online via the community whom you now communicate personally with, either by email, telephone or face-to-face?
Membership	How would you describe your initial presence in the community? Did you feel you were an outsider sitting on the edge observing? How did this change? What changed it?
Pedagogy	Have your teaching practices changed as a result from what you have learnt in the community?
Problem solving	Do you use the online community as a problem solving resource? If so, has it been useful? Do you consider this to be an important role?
Continuous Professional Development	Is the on-going continuous nature of online communities an advantage? Why?
Professional communication	In your opinion, is professional discussion valuable? How is participating in professional discussions online different or better than professional discussions in your workplace?
Professional Development	Do you feel membership to an online professional community, like the one you belong to, represents a worthwhile form of professional development?

Data Analysis

Data analysis was conducted on all three instruments, that is, community discussion transcripts, an electronic survey questionnaire and the transcripts from the focus group forum. The details of the tools used to conduct the analysis will be discussed further.

Community transcripts

In Chapter 2 the literature review pertaining to electronic surveys in qualitative research was presented. The content analysis framework used in this study was the *Practical Inquiry Model* developed by Garrison, Anderson and Archer (2001). This model recognises and incorporates the shared world and the private world of an individual as important components in the construction of knowledge. This is highly applicable to online Communities of Practice due to the shared/private world perspective. Members participating in online discussions are motivated by experiences in their private world. This framework manages to incorporate the social construction of knowledge and the place of the individual within that learning landscape.

The model is divided into four phases; triggering event, exploration, integration and resolution. These phases attempt to reflect the critical thinking process learners engage in when constructing knowledge (Garrison et al., 2001). These four phases each contain a descriptor, which in effect acts as the broadest grouping of codes. This is demonstrated in Figure 3.4. The descriptor codes are indicative of the type of activities the learner is engaged in within that phase. In the triggering event, messages are coded as *Evocative* they are essentially evoking a discussion. There are three codes within this descriptor that represent the different types of evocative message. In the exploration phase, messages are coded as *Inquisitive* as they are concerned with inquiry and clarification. There are six codes within this descriptor. In the integration phase, messages are coded as *Tentative* as they represent attempts to synthesis and to reach a consensus regarding a discussion topic. There are four codes within this descriptor. The final phase, resolution, has three *Committed* codes and these messages clearly identify that a solution or resolution has been reached.

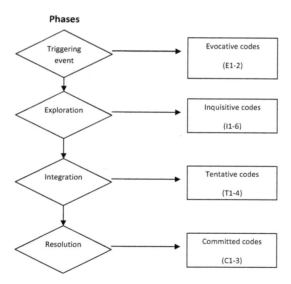

Figure 3.4: Phases and descriptors of *The Practical Inquiry Model*

(Garrison et al., 2001)

51

As mentioned above, each descriptor contains a number of possible codes for messages, which Garrison et al. (2001) describe as Indicators. These indicators or different types of messages within the descriptor are presented in greater detail in Figures 3.5 – 3.8 (Garrison et al., 2001). Evocative messages were triggering messages that initiated a new community discussion. The types of messages that could be coded within this descriptor can be seen in Figure 3.5.

Descriptor	Indicators	Sociocognitive Processes	Code
Evocative	Recognising the problem	Presenting background information that results in a question	E1
	Sense of puzzlement	Asking questions	E2

Figure 3.5: Triggering Events

Inquisitive messages were concerned with exploring, clarifying and initially responding to an evocative message. These types of messages largely occurred early in a discussion. The types of messages that could be coded within this descriptor can be seen in Figure 3.6.

Descriptor	Indicators	Sociocognitive Processes	Code
Inquisitive	Divergence – within the online community	Unsubstantiated contradiction of previous ideas	I1
	Divergence – within a single message	Many different ideas/themes presented in one message	I2
	Information exchange	Personal narratives/descriptions/facts (not used as evidence to support a conclusion)	I3
	Suggestions for consideration	Author explicitly characterises message as exploration – e.g. "Does that seem right?"	I4
	Brainstorming	Adds to established points but does not systematically defend/justify/develop addition	I5
	Leaps to conclusions	Offers unsupported opinions	I6

Figure 3.6: Exploration

Tentative messages displayed attempts to reach a consensus or a solution within the discussion. There was a sense of building on or linking together contributions made by other members during the course of the discussion. The types of messages that could be coded within this descriptor can be seen in Figure 3.7.

Descriptor	Indicators	Sociocognitive Processes	Code
Tentative	Convergence – among group members	Reference to previous message followed by substantiated agreement. Building on, adding to other's ideas	T1
	Convergence – within a single message	Justified, developed, defensible, yet tentative hypothesis	T2
	Connecting ideas, synthesis	Integrating information from various sources.	T3
	Creating solutions	Explicit characterisation of message as a solution by participant	T4

Figure 3.7: Integration

The final phase, resolution, contained committed messages. These were messages that resolved the discussion, such as selecting a solution or applying a solution to an authentic context. The types of messages that could be coded within this descriptor can be seen in Figure 3.8.

Descriptor	Indicators	Sociocognitive Processes	Code
Committed	Vicarious application to real world	None	C1
	Testing solutions	Coded	C2
	Defending solutions		C3

Figure 3.8: Resolution

The unit that was coded, was the message itself, as Henri (1990) suggested, each message has its own meaning and can be considered on its own (p.118). A message posted during an online discussion or posted to a noticeboard in response to a discussion thread, is generally limited to one topic. It was expected that some messages could be classified into more than one category; those messages will be classified based on primacy to ensure reliability.

As mentioned previously, the community transcripts were electronic documents accessed via community archives. Thus it was decided to preserve the integrity of these documents by coding them electronically. The messages were coded using the qualitative software program MAXqda2®. The transcript analysis is presented in detail in Chapter 5.

Survey

The electronic survey provided a large amount of data that initially need to be sorted into manageable units. Miles and Huberman (1994) viewed qualitative analysis as consisting of three stages; data reduction, data display and conclusion drawing and verification. The analysis of the survey followed these three phases.

- *Data reduction*

The raw data was collected as *Excel®* spreadsheets and contained a mixture of open and closed responses. The open responses were broad and difficult to comprehend in their raw form hence there was a need to employ data reduction techniques. Data reduction "refers to the process of selecting, focusing, simplifying, abstracting and transforming data" (Miles & Huberman, 1994, p. 10). Themes and commonalities were initially sought and raw data was grouped under these categories. This allowed the researcher to determine general consensus regarding a question.

- *Data Display*

The data display stage was when the data is "an organised, compressed assembly of information that permits conclusion drawing and action" (Miles & Huberman, 1994, p. 11). Much of the data from the closed questions was tabulated and this format permitted easier understanding of meaning and allowed for contrast and comparison of results. The data from the open questions was further reduced after careful analysis into sub-categories and themes. The information collected by the electronic survey was further analysed using the statistical program SPSS®. The data was presented graphically in tables in order to determine if relationships existed between variables. The data submitted to analysis via SPSS® was comprised mainly of demographical information and opinions elicited using a rating scale. This phase is presented in detail in Chapter 4.

- *Conclusion drawing and verification*

The final stage of analysis that was applied to the survey was conclusion drawing and verification. Miles and Huberman (1994) stated that conclusions need to be verified meanings emerging from the data have to be *tested* for their plausibility, their sturdiness, their "confirmability" – that is, their *validity* (p. 11). The conclusions reached regarding the data collected by the survey are presented in detail in Chapter 4. These conclusions were further verified by the data collected by the transcripts and forum and this is presented in Chapter 6.

Forum

The analysis of the transcripts from the focus group forum were submitted to analysis guided by the phases outlined above by Miles and Huberman (1994) in Chapter 3.

- *Data reduction*

The focus group forum was conducted electronically and hence the data was collected and stored as electronic documents. Due to the structure of the forum, the data was stored as eight separate documents and these 'chunks' of data were subject specific and pertained to one question and its resulting discussion. Hence the initial data reduction was performed by the structure of the forum itself. These were then submitted to broad analysis for themes and commonalities in messages. This allowed the researcher to determine the general consensus regarding a question.

- *Data Display*

This phase of the analysis was concerned with organising the data into a format that permits conclusion drawing and action (Miles & Huberman, 1994, p.11). The data collected was organised into two frameworks. The first framework for analysis utilised the initial grouping of the transcripts around each discussion topic (see Table 3.2). This was surveyed for themes and commonalities which formed secondary headings. The individual messages were then grouped together under secondary headings. This permitted a clearer understanding of the general opinions of the group and the responses to the questions.

The second framework for analysis involved separating the answers into profiles for each of the participants (*n*=11). This was aimed at creating a sense of individual members and their concerns. These profiles were interesting from a personal insight perspective, as a clearer impression of individual members was able to be developed. The unit of analysis was again, the message itself which has been previously justified above.

During the separating of data into the two frameworks, the researcher also employed a technique suggested by Miles and Huberman (1994) called tactics for generating meaning (p.245). This required the researcher to step back and systematically examine and re-examine the data guided by 13 strategies. These strategies guide the researcher to notice patterns, make comparisons and note relationships between variables. These strategies were employed to generate meaning from the messages and help develop a clearer understanding of the subject being discussed.

- *Conclusion drawing and verification*

The final phase of analysis that was applied to the forum was conclusion drawing and verification. As mentioned previously, the forum was used as a tool to clarify and elucidate themes or issues that arose from the survey and transcript analysis. It also was a tool to verify the conclusions reached in the data analysis of these two phases. Hence the conclusions drawn and their verification are presented in detail in Chapter 6.

Validity and reliability

The tactics that were used to increase the validity and reliability of this study included:

- The use of data (community transcripts) that were unsolicited by the researcher and are thus unbiased and not influenced by the aims of the study.
- The use of appropriate analysis techniques that reflected the nature of the data collected
- Use of a combination of open and closed questions that enabled respondents to clarify or provide their own answers if none were suitable.
- Pilot testing the survey on a control group of teachers with adjustments made based on feedback.
- Sampling a wide variety of teachers, not limited to a particular state or county or teaching background.
- The use of data collection techniques that complimented the propositions of the research.

When conducting a qualitative study it is important that the validity and reliability of the conclusions are verified. This can be achieved via triangulation "the process of using multiple perceptions to clarify meaning, verifying the repeatability of an observation or interpretation"

(Stake, 2003, p. 148). Triangulation was achieved via conducting the data collection in phases. Phase 1 and 2, after initial analysis informed the construction of the data instrument used in Phase 3. The conclusions drawn after analysis of the survey were supported by evidence found in the transcript analysis and the focus group forum. This is clearly demonstrated in the synthesis of findings presented in Chapter 6.

Summary

In conclusion, the methodology presented in this chapter has attempted to find a balance between the unique nature of the cases and subjects, that is patterns of participation and the members of online communities and the focus of the study. This study has been designed as a multiple case study (Creswell, 2005) and has sought to investigate online communities as a source of professional development for teachers. The collective cases investigated were the participation and involvement of members in the activities hosted by three online communities of practice. Three communities were selected, one state, national and international, to provide a range of professional and geographical environments. This provided a wider scope for the study and ensured a cross-profession perspective.

4. Findings: Online Survey

We communicate to express ourselves, to transmit information and to learn

(Hoadley & Pea, 2002, p.323)

Overview

Electronic communication is characteristically concerned with 'the message'(eM), those who send them (S) and those who receive and read them (R). This relationship could be simplified into the equation $eM = S + R$. When this simple equation is applied to online communities several elements are added that make this simple act of sending and receiving a message more complex. These new elements are characteristics such as asynchronicity, unknown senders and readers, non-linear text and the absence of non-verbal cues. The equation modifies itself from being a simple communicative act to one that has the potential not only to inform, but to transform. The electronic message in an online community may be a request for help or information, the offering of ideas and solutions or the contemplation of an issue. What is apparent is that the complexity of these messages lies in their impact outside the online environment. It is apparent from the messages themselves that the information is being applied to real, authentic contexts and is not limited to the online environment. In order to understand this complexity, the data collection will focus on the electronic messages of the three online communities involved in the study, the members who sent them and their content.

The discussion in this chapter is concerned with the findings of the electronic survey open to members of all three online communities and designed to provide information about *who* the members of these communities are and what they hope to achieve through their membership. This discussion needs to be prefaced with an understanding of the populations from which the data has been drawn. Table 4.1 presents a summary of the three online communities under review.

Table 4.1

Teacher online communities

Community Name	Acronym	Specialisation	Membership (as at Jan 2006)	Physical Location	Year founded
BECTA Top Teachers	BECTA	Implementing and using ICTs in the classroom	568	UK	2002
Oz-TeacherNet	OTN	General community list - pedagogical and professional issues affecting teachers	608	QUT, Brisbane Australia	1995
SSABSA English Teachers	SSABSA	Teachers of English	112	Adelaide	2003

The potential total population for this study was large (*N*=1288) and, while predominantly Australian, had representation from a number of different countries. The total membership of the communities, however, is not a reliable measure of the study population as it can be presumed that active membership would represent only 20-30% of the population, this figure was reached by counting the number of messages per member, per community over three months and then averaging the tally. A more realistic estimate of likely participants would be 250-400 people. Similarly, while it cannot be known with any surety, it can be supposed that the members of these communities are teachers or involved directly or indirectly with education and schooling.

It can be said, however, that the members of these communities as subjects for this study represented a genuine cross-section of nationalities, systems and ages. Neither were they were limited to a particular teaching area or to a particular geographical location. This diversity allowed an interesting snapshot of how professional development for teachers is generally offered and organised. It also identified that there were some similarities in teacher problems and needs that were common across the profession.

Online Survey

The purpose of the online survey was to gather demographic data and provide insight into the professional development experiences, attitudes and skills of the members of online teacher professional communities. An open invitation to participate was sent to all members of the three online communities (see Table 4.1) reviewed in this study. This invitation was extended through an email to the respective lists which included a URL link to the survey hosted by QUT. Ninety-eight members responded to the invitation by completing the survey, irrespective of personal experience, country or system.

The survey was available for three weeks and members were sent a 'reminder' email encouraging them to participate after the first two weeks had elapsed. The survey had a consent mechanism built into the first page where respondents recorded their consent to participate in the research by selecting the 'Start Survey' button. All responses were anonymous and no personal details such as email or IP addresses were collected thereby ensuring privacy. This means that the respondents (n = 98) could not be identified and no data is therefore available to determine from which community the respondents originate.

The survey comprised of a combination of 25 open and closed questions (See Appendix 1) organised around four topics. These were (a) background (b) professional development, (c) online communities, and (d) ICT use. For purposes of clarity and organisation, the findings will be presented through these four topics.

Background

The background topic contained five closed questions designed to collect broad demographical information about the members of the online community. This topic was specifically designed to build a profile of the members of these professional online communities based on age, gender, area/level of teaching, number of years experience and level of confidence with ICTs. It is important to note that the results collected by the survey are not necessarily representative of communities in general but is limited to those concerned with teaching and teachers. A further consideration to note is that the results represent those who positively responded to the invitation to participate and are not necessarily indicative of the teaching profession per se. They present as a valid snapshot of life online and represent the experiences of these people and not the profession in general. Table 4.2 presents a summary of the gender and age characteristics of the survey respondents which shows, as with the general population of teachers, a preponderance of females (81.63%) over males (18.37%).

Table 4.2

Gender of survey respondents sorted by age

Age	20-29 n (%)	30-39 n (%)	40-49 n (%)	50-59 n (%)	60+ n (%)	Total n (%)
Male	1 (1.02%)	3 (3.06%)	5 (5.1%)	9 (9.18%)	0 (0%)	18 (18.37%)
Female	6 (6.12%)	11 (11.22%)	22 (22.45%)	36 (36.73%)	5 (5.1%)	80 (81.63%)
Total	7 (7.14%)	14 (14.29%)	27 (27.55%)	45 (45.92%)	5 (5.1%)	98 (100%)

As can be discerned from Table 4.2 and seen in Figure 4.1, the majority of respondents to the online survey were female (81.63%) and were predominantly aged between 40 – 59 years (with 22.45% aged from 40-49 years and 36.73% aged between 50-59 years). This would appear to be fairly indicative of gender trends in teaching, with the total number of teachers who are female represents 67.96% of teaching staff and males representing 32.04% (ABS, 2005). The distribution is also indicative of trends, with the majority of teachers in Australia (63%) falling within the 35-44 years and 45-54 years age groups (ABS, 2003). The youngest age group responding to the survey was the 20-29 year old cohort and this proved to be a small group (*n*=7, representing 7.14% of all survey respondents) but again predominantly female. This would be expected as according to ABS (2003) fewer young people are entering the teaching profession and the median age of teachers has risen from 34 (in 1991) to 43 (in 2003). The lowest response rate was from the 60+ group (*n*=5, representing 5.1% of all survey respondents) where all respondents were female.

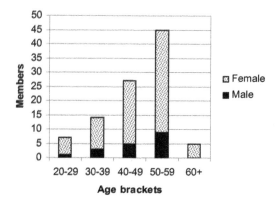

Figure 4.1   Age of survey respondents sorted by age

61

The majority of respondents to the online survey (n=98) came from a primary school teaching background (n=32, 32.65%) with teacher librarians (n=28, 28.57%) and secondary teachers (n=27, 27.55%) well and quite equally represented. The groups which were not well represented in the survey were (a) early childhood (n=3, 3.06%), (b) tertiary (n=1, 1.02%), and (c) adult/vocational educators (n=1, 1.02%). This lower representation might indicate (a) that the ICT skills of teachers working in these areas may not be as proficient; or (b) teachers in these areas do not feel the need for support; or (c) that teachers in these areas may subscribe to area-specific online communities rather than the "general" teaching communities under review in this study.

A further six respondents (6.12%) selected the "other" option. It would appear that these responses were from experienced teachers who had moved in to more senior positions within the teaching field. Details offered in clarification were (a) professional development, (b) cross-sector teaching (2 instances), (c) senior project officer for government department, (d) special education teacher and (e) Catholic education officer.

A gender breakdown according to teaching area can be seen in Table 4.3. This shows that the largest group to respond to the survey were female primary teachers (28.57%), followed by female teacher librarians (25.51%) and female secondary teachers (18.37%). As noted, there was a noticeable difference between the number of male and female teachers who responded to the survey, but the largest group of male teachers were secondary teachers (9.18%).

Table 4.3

Breakdown of gender and teaching area

Teaching area	Male n (%)	Female n (%)	Total n (%)
Early Childhood	1 (1.02%)	2 (2.04%)	3 (3.06%)
Primary	4 (4.08%)	28 (28.57%)	32 (32.65%)
Secondary	9 (9.18%)	18 (18.37%)	27 (27.55%)
Tertiary	0 (0%)	1 (1.02%)	1 (1.02%)
Adult/Vocational	0 (0%)	1 (1.02%)	1 (1.02%)
Teacher Librarian	3 (3.06%)	25 (25.51%)	28 (28.57%)
Other	1 (1.02%)	5 (5.1%)	6 (6.12%)
Total	18 (18.37 %)	80 (61.63%)	98 (100.00%)

The respondents represented a group of highly experienced teachers with the majority having over 20 years experience (n=59, representing 60.2% of all survey respondents) which is consistent in relation to the largest age cohort being 50-59 years of age (45.92%) (see Table 4.2 and Figure 4.1). The number of years of teaching experience ranked after 20+ years and from largest grouping to the least were 11-15 years (12.24%), 1-5 years (10.2%), 16-20 years (9.18%) and 6-10 years (8.16%). These four groups, although considerably smaller than the 20+ years group, were comparably represented with the spread ranging from 8-13%. As the majority of respondents (n=59, N=98) had over 20 years of teaching experience, it might be concluded that this group represents experienced confident members of their online communities.

Respondents to the survey were asked to rate their own level of confidence in using ICTs from a pre-defined and hierarchical list of descriptors. These were (a) very poor (no response), (b) poor (n=1, 1.02%), (c) competent (n=26, 26.53%), (d) highly competent (n=34, 34.69%), and (e) professionally competent (n=37, 37.76%). The responses therefore ranged from competent to professionally competent (98.08%) with only one respondent (1.02%) indicating a poor level of confidence in using ICT. Seventy-one respondents (72.45%) indicated a confidence level which was either highly or professionally competent.

This high level of perception of capacity would be expected as the survey respondents represent a group who have independently sought out an online environment – an action which demands both competence and confidence. The one respondent who indicated a poor level of confidence, upon closer examination, had the following profile:

- Female
- Aged 40-49 years
- Primary school teacher
- 16-20 years teaching experience
- Member of online community for 1-3 years.

This might indicate that the respondent is actively trying to improve her ICT skills by seeking out online communities and thereby engaging in opportunities to practise those skills or she may have self-rated her ICT skills harshly. Alternatively she might epitomise the legitimate peripheral participant described by Wenger (1998) who is trying to make the transition to a more experienced and confident member of the online community of practice. The mismatch in her years of teaching and her years of online membership support the hypothesis of a person using the list for her own professional development.

In order to determine if there was a relationship between the number of years of teaching experience and the respondents' level of confidence in using ICTs, these two variables were cross tabulated using Pearson's chi-square. A summary of these findings can be seen in Table 4.4.

Table 4.4

*No. of years teaching experience * Level of confidence using ICTs*

		Level of confidence using ICTs				Total
		Poor	Competent	Highly competent	Professionally competent	
No. of years teaching experience	1-5 years	0	2	4	4	10
	6-10 years	0	0	4	4	8
	11-15 years	0	3	5	4	12
	16-20 years	1	5	2	1	9
	20+ years	0	16	19	24	59
	Total	1	26	34	37	98

These results allow us to conclude, as previously noted, that the teachers who responded to the survey (n=98) were generally an ICT competent group of professionals. At the lower end of the confidence scale (poor to competent) were generally teachers with over 10 years of experience. Confidence in ICT was particularly well represented by teachers with over 20 years of teaching experience. The results of the Pearson chi-square analysis of Table 4.4 revealed that there was no explicit relationship between these two variables: Pearson χ^2 (1, N = 98) = 18.566, $p <$ 0.100.

Two further factors, namely, the area currently working in and the level of confidence in using ICTs were submitted to the same analysis. As seen in Table 4.5, the most confident teachers in the use of ICTs were from a primary background, followed by teacher librarians and secondary teachers. These three groups stood out clearly from the other teaching areas, achieving scores for their level of confidence in using ICTs ranging from 27 – 32 in total (see Totals column in Table 4.5). There was a dramatic difference with the next grouping which dropped to only 6 (Early Childhood). An explanation for this result may be (a) the types of learning activities these teachers create, (b) the resources available at their schools or due to (c) the expectations of staff and students. The results of the Pearson chi-square analysis of Table 4.5 revealed that there was a small probability of a significant relationship between these two variables: Pearson χ^2 (1, N = 98) =

64

18.020, $p < 0.454$. This score is insufficient to conclude that an influence exists between the numbers of years of teaching experience being related to the level of confidence in the use of ICTs.

Table 4.5

*Area currently working in * Level of confidence using ICTs*

		Level of confidence using ICTs				Total
		Poor	Competent	Highly competent	Professionally competent	
Teaching Area/Level	Early Childhood	0	1	2	0	3
	Primary	1	9	15	7	32
	Secondary	0	5	10	12	27
	Tertiary	0	0	1	0	1
	Adult/ Vocational	0	0	0	1	1
	Teacher Librarian	0	10	4	14	28
	Other	0	1	2	3	6
	Total	1	26	34	37	98

From the findings that have been presented so far in relation to the background section of the online survey, we can conclude that the average respondent to the online survey was female, aged between 50-59 years and working in the primary sector. The respondents generally have over 20 years of teaching experience and they are professionally competent in using ICT.

Professional Development

The professional development section of the online survey contained 7 questions (2 open, 1 ranking, 4 closed). This section of the survey was designed to explore the professional development (PD) experiences of the members and elicit personal opinions and suggestions regarding this topic. The questions were also designed to explore some of the interim conclusions reached in the literature review (Chapter 2) regarding professional development and teachers. The findings from these questions are reported in the following subsections relating to each of the questions asked about PD in general.

Respondents' PD experiences

The respondents were asked to describe their PD experiences both on-line and off-line over the previous 12 months. The majority of responses could be categorised as being conferences, workshops and courses. Some of these were compulsory such as first aid certification, mandatory government policy or initiative training sessions and syllabus sessions. Courses or workshops that attracted favourable comments were generally subject-specific and thus personally relevant. This demand for authentic and contextualised professional development is consistent with the findings of Lloyd and Cochrane (2006) who suggested that context is of one four elements (along with time, professional growth and community) critical in effective professional development.

A particular type of course or training that received favourable comments tended to be any associated with technology, for example, digital animation, *MovieMaker*®, *Excel*® workshops, *INTEL*®, website development or using the Internet in the classroom. This keen commentary on technology-based training is not unexpected from a cohort who are active members of online communities and thus could be considered highly interested in ICTs. Another form of PD highly valued were conferences. The benefits of attending conferences were identified as networking and meeting peers from around the country and were further praised as engaging, exciting and innovative.

Respondents were also asked to describe any particular program that left a favourable impression and to offer an explanation. These were specifically-named courses and were selected for a variety of reasons. Most of these can be grouped together and can be characterised as programs that:

(a) presented different strategies that can be implemented in the classroom;

(b) exposed them to new ideas and techniques by a specialist from a particular area;

(c) allowed them to participate and be creative; and,

(d) allowed them to present as well as observe.

For example, four respondents mentioned a peer-tutoring program that had been established in their schools, where staff were learning from each other by engaging in project-based ICT lessons each week.

There were also some negative comments made about PD experiences with descriptive criticisms and emotive phrases used as descriptors, namely, compulsory, boring, "chalk and talk", irrelevant, irregular and disorganised. Some respondents voluntarily offered additional information regarding how they sought out PD opportunities themselves, outside of school requirements, but it was not explained why they felt the need to do so. The types of PD they independently sought were professional chat groups (Edtalk, IT-teachers), M.Ed courses, personal skill development courses (software programs), refresher courses, professional reading (journals) and membership to online communities.

Employers' PD requirements

The second open question asked respondents to comment on their employer's PD requirements per year. This question was divided into two sections. Firstly, respondents were asked to comment on attendance, that is, if it was compulsory or voluntary and if they were required to meet a PD quota per year. Secondly, they were asked for their impression of the PD requirements mandated by their current employer. This mix of formal and informal professional learning experiences is of interest to this study as it would offer insight into the forms of professional learning teachers seek out.

The majority of the respondents reported that they were required to fulfil or at least demonstrate that they had achieved a certain number of PD hours per year. There was a broad range of answers which defied comparative analysis. These included 37.5 hours per year, 2 weeks compulsory PD sessions, 30 credit points per year (with 1 credit point equal to 1 hour), 40 hours, a combination of 2 departmental days, 2 school-based days and 1 day of own choice, 6 hours per year, and 3 hours per week. Additionally, teachers working within particular education authorities such as Catholic Education Australia had additional PD requirements of 20 hours in Religious Education. Amidst this were some reports of no mandated quota or specified programs of professional development. This indicates that employer demands range dramatically within the profession and between systems and geographic locations and supports a conclusion that there is no overarching system of measurement.

Generally those respondents who were working within a PD quota seemed positive about this requirement. Some, however, responded that the mandated requirements made PD tedious, irrelevant, insufficient and "open to rorting." There was also criticism about the types of PD some staff selected in order to satisfy the quota with one respondent describing this as "Mickey mouse type PD" that is, selected to meet the quota of hours rather than to meet specific needs. It would also appear that, for the majority of respondents, meeting the quota had a built-in incentive such as taking "Week 41" as paid leave rather than spending an additional week at school in Term 4.

The presence of a quota did not appear to constrain the amount of time the respondents spent per year on PD. Many respondents reported that they sought further courses outside of (additional to) the quota or the required PD program and set themselves PD quotas based on specific areas, for example, 25 hours of ICT PD per year and several respondents reported reaching between 100-200 hours per year. It could be contended that this group are not typical and that they represent a highly motivated and professionally responsible cohort as evidenced by their membership to online communities. They could simply be of a mindset that seeks out those types of opportunities – a prime example of this being the previously cited female primary teacher who, despite having indicated a poor level of confidence, was an active member of her community list. Whether they are indicative of the profession as a whole would need to be examined further.

Financial constraints also affected the amount of time and the type of PD that respondents selected. It would appear that teachers had restricted access to funding for PD and the availability of funds has not been standardised across systems and sectors. Some respondents reported that their schools were very happy to provide funding for courses whilst others were limited to fixed amounts from $100-200 per year. The largest group were those who had to pay for professional development courses out of their own money. This had an effect of limiting what they would do with one respondent stating that "$600 [at own expense per year] is enough, after that I don't go." This appears to represent a problem as some teachers are required to meet a PD quota but, as their school or education authorities do not provide them with PD opportunities, they must seek alternatives themselves which often incur costs. This may explain the attraction of online communities as a source of PD as teachers are making use of existing and freely available networks to meet quotas or needs.

Decision making

The respondents were asked who, in their opinion, would be the most appropriate person(s) to decide on the content of the PD programs they undertook and they were permitted to select more than one answer from a given list. The consensus was that teaching staff (87.75%) themselves were the most suitable. This finding appears to be supported by Richardson's (1990) findings which concluded that, for PD to successfully result in changes to teaching practices and to be more positively received, teachers should be included in the planning and design stages. Two options for decision-making, School Administration and Department Heads, received similar scores (28.57% and 29.59% respectively) and so did not indicate a particular preference. Only 20.40% believed that education authorities should determine the PD activities of teachers while 3.06% of responses were given to an unspecified "other".

The respondents who selected "Other" with regard to who was the most appropriate to decide on the content of PD programs offered a number of alternatives. These suggestions can be grouped loosely into three categories: (a) external groups, (b) the individual, and (c) combinations. The responses grouped under the title (a) external groups included professional bodies such as the Institute of Biology, advisors, professional associations and universities. Most of these suggestions might have fit under the option "Education Authorities" in the survey but the respondents appeared to choose to clarify their response by selecting "Other". Under the grouping (b) the individual were suggestions such as self-generated PD with teachers identifying what they need, individual, and being able to freely select from a variety of courses. These suggestions could have belonged to the option "Teaching staff" but what is clear is that there is an emphasis on the individual self-determining their learning and conducting it by themselves. This raises issues such as freedom of choice and personalised learning which might be absent from current PD programs.

Finally, the last grouping of suggestions (c) combinations contained suggestions such as working collaboratively to make the decision, "a mix of all," and "all should be involved to provide breadth." These responses suggest that a number of options have a potential role to play in the PD of teachers but perhaps the current structure or system does not harness that potential fully. It would appear that the survey respondents were suggesting a more coordinated approach to PD. Under the "combinations" grouping, it was also suggested that there should be a committee comprising staff from all faculties and executive or a teacher committee which liaises with principals. This suggestion once again reiterates the need to provide teachers with a "voice" regarding the content and form of PD programs which appears to be lacking or is perceived to be lacking at present.

Preferred learning methods

The respondents were asked to select their preferred learning method and the results can be seen in Table 4.6. The respondents to the survey indicated a clear preference for face-to-face courses with these being ranked in the top two positions and representing over half (53.05%) of all responses.

Table 4.6

Preferred learning method (in descending order)

Method of learning	% (N=98)
Learning with your colleagues face-to-face not from your workplace	28.57
Learning with your colleagues face-to-face from your workplace	24.48
Learning individually and electronically	21.42
Learning with an anonymous group of colleagues electronically	10.20
Learning individually, in a course conducted away from your workplace	9.18
Other	6.12
Learning with your colleagues from your workplace electronically	2.04

Given that these teachers were responding through an online survey based around online communities and as mentioned previously, represented a cross-section of teachers who actively engage in online learning and who display a high level of ICT competency, it was expected that "online" options would prove popular. However, methods that involved face-to-face contact received 53.05% of the answers while electronically-based methods received a combined response of only 33.66%. This result is consistent with other findings that conclude teachers learn best collaboratively, face-to-face (Boyle et al., 2004; Goldenberg & Gallimore, 1991; Huberman, 2001; Kemmis, 1989) but which may be unreliable in the inherent ambiguity of the options and the loose definition of terms. It might also be conjectured that the respondents to the survey perceived "learning" to be formal rather than informal learning.

From the responses to this item, it would appear that the most popular method of learning is face-to-face contact with a group of colleagues who were not from their workplace (28.57%). This may indicate that teachers need the opportunity to communicate with a group of professional peers and that they need broader social interaction that can be provided from within their workplace.

The responses which included the term "colleagues" drew 65.29% of all responses irrespective of whether this was face-to-face or electronic. This would indicate that teachers respond best to socially constructed knowledge. It might also reflect the desire for a community-based approach to learning (Watts & Castle, 1992) or the desire for professional support.

The majority of PD programs experienced by the respondents would largely have been face-to-face short courses or single sessions usually conducted at school by an outside expert. Thus perceiving their membership to an online community as a form of PD requires a conceptual shift in their understanding of professional learning. Teachers prior experienced may have resulted in pre-conceived ideas about how PD should be structured. The need for contact between peers not from their workplace is something they are achieving in their online communities, the fact that they have not made the leap from this type of contact to it being a context for PD might be a contextually and conceptually-based problem of perception rather than it being perceived as unsuitable. The finding may also reflect poor experiences of the type of PD pejoratively called "PD on a CD" where self-paced course material has been distributed for teachers to work through in their own time. The perception may be that all "electronic" PD uses this delivery as opposed to a communication model.

Six respondents (n=98) to this item selected "other" but there were 14 open responses to this question as some respondents felt the need to explain their choice. A clear indication of preference was given for learning with any group away from the workplace which indicates a desire to be on more neutral ground or the need to be removed from daily practice in order to take a new perspective. The suggestions made for team, faculty and interdisciplinary-based learning were still indicative of a preference for face-to-face and collegial learning but might also be seen to be a comment on the content of the program and therefore consistent with the previous finding that teachers themselves felt they should make decisions about PD programs.

Six respondents (*n*=98) indicated that all of the options had a place depending on the topic or goal of the program. Another respondent proposed that the learning needs to be workplace-based but could take any form, either individually, with colleagues or electronically. This desire to keep PD workplace-based may indicate a need for the content to be authentic and closely-related to the everyday practices of teachers which has been suggested by research (Guskey, 2002; Lloyd & Cochrane, 2006; Richardson, 1990). Finally, a suggestion was made by four respondents that the options described could all be supplemented with online learning. This might indicate these respondents saw online learning playing a support or resource role in their professional development rather than being the environment in which to learn.

PD locations

The respondents were asked to indicate their preference for a location for PD. There was a clear preference for locations away from the workplace with only 29.59% preferring to have PD based in their school. The findings for this item, presented in Table 4.7, are consistent with findings for the previous item where a similarly clear preference was indicated for learning to be (a) with others not known to the respondent and (b) not in the respondent's workplace. This is an interesting preference and appears to be contradictory to situated learning theory, which suggested that learning needed to be situated in an authentic situation (that is, their workplace) or the knowledge created would be false (Brown et al., 1989). It would also appear contradictory to statements made by respondents regarding the aims of PD and their preference for authenticity and contextual relevancy. Perhaps the attraction of locations away from school is just that, the desire to be away from their normal work environment.

Table 4.7
Preferred location for PD (in descending order)

Location	% (*N*=98)
In a neutral environment (e.g. convention room)	40.82
At school / workplace	29.59
Other	11.22
At home via the Internet	10.2
At a higher education provider (e.g. University, Technical College)	8.16

There were 21 contributions made to the 'other' option for this question though only 11 respondents (*n*=98) selected this choice. The majority of the comments were clarifying why a particular choice was made, for example, "I chose school because of time constraints" indicating a low attraction for programs that require the teacher to be away from school. Of the comments made, 7 respondents suggested that all of the choices were suitable but were dependent on the nature of the PD program. Some suggestions named specific PD providers such as City Learning Centre (United Kingdom) whilst some commented that some options had a "double" meaning, for example, "a neutral environment is also online."

Duration of PD

The respondents were asked what duration PD should be if it were to achieve real change to teaching practices (see Table 4.8). The short program (2-3 months) option received the highest score (40.82%) followed by short single sessions (1-2 hours) (22.44%) and longer programs (6 months +) (20.41%).

Table 4.8

Duration of PD to affect change (in descending order)

Location	% (N=98)
Short programs (e.g. 2-3 months)	40.82
Short single sessions (1-2 hours)	22.44
Longer programs (e.g. 6 months +)	20.41
Other	16.33

This result supports research that has suggested short single sessions are not popular with teachers (Garet et al., 2001) nor that they achieve any real change to teaching practices (Sorge & Russell, 2000). However short single sessions still ranked quite highly (second), perhaps the respondents perceive this type of session effective for a particular role such as acquiring a new skill or information about a new policy.

The comments made in the "other" option might explain this further. A high number of respondents chose this option (16.33%) with the majority of answers able to be grouped under a loose "all options - depends on activity" heading. Some of the suggestions indicated a personalised approach to be adopted with the duration depending on the individual teacher and their needs. This desire for a more personalised PD program has been identified by a number of researchers (Franke et al., 1998; Gallimore et al., 1986; Richardson, 1992) and has similarly emerged in the findings of this survey particularly in the responses to questions about decision making.

Four respondents commented that the most effective model for change was "continuous and ongoing" PD and that this "is the real benefit of [learning] online." This type of PD, that is, continuous and ongoing, can be facilitated easily by online methods, but this method appears to be contradictory to the identified "face-to-face, colleagues not from workplace and conducted away from workplace" criteria determined by the responses to the previous two questions. There was one negative comment in response to this question where the respondent offered that "none of these models effects change" but no alternative was suggested.

Aims of PD

The final question in this section asked respondents to rank 8 statements regarding the aims of PD. The statements were collected from the conclusions suggested by research conducted on PD and teachers. The statements (in rank order) are presented in the table below, which clearly indicates the research associated with each statement.

Table 4.9

The aims of PD supported by references from literature

Statements regarding the aims of PD (ranked in perceived importance by respondents)	Reference
1. Positive change to teaching practice	Borko et al., 1997; Franke et al., 1998; Hawkes, 1997; Hoadley & Pea, 2002; Marx, Blumenfeld & Krajcik, 1998; Richardson, 1990
2. An improvement in student learning	Guskey 2002; Richardson, 1990
3. Obtaining new skills or knowledge	Huberman, 2001; Stehle, Whatley, Kurz & Hausfather, 2001; Richardson, 1990
4. Creating a supportive learning environment within the workplace	Billet, 1993; Hodkinson & Hodkinson, 2002; Huberman, 2001; Ingvarson, Meiers & Beavis, 2003
5. Solving problems encountered in the	Franke et al., 1998; Richardson, 1990

classroom	
6. Updating theoretical knowledge	Borko et al., 1997; Gallimore, Dalton & Tharp, 1986; Richardson, 1990; 1992; 1994; 1997; Richardson & Placier, 2001
7. Forging closer bonds with colleagues	Goldenberg & Gallimore, 1991; Sorge & Russell, 2000
8. Increasing teacher motivation and enthusiasm	Borko & Putnam, 1995; Richardson, 1990

The statement ranked first, "Positive change to teaching practice" achieved 34.69% of the responses followed closely by the second-ranked statement "An improvement in student learning" which achieved 33.67% of all responses (n=98). These two aims would appear to be highly valued by the respondents to this survey and also more broadly to teachers who are looking for evidence of positive change to student learning (Guskey, 2002) before new skills or knowledge learnt are adopted and result in change to teaching practice (Guskey, 2002; Richardson, 1990).

The positioning of "Obtaining new skills or knowledge" in third position confirms the comments collected in previous questions in the survey that describes this as a key outcome of PD and that teaching is constantly changing and new ideas are being continually disseminated throughout the profession. If we examine the lowest ranking statements "Forging closer bonds with colleagues" and "Increasing motivation and enthusiasm," it is interesting – and somewhat contradictory - to note that these are two of the most highly commented on positive attributes of membership to an online community by respondents. Without further opportunity to interview survey respondents, this disparity remains an interesting contradiction in teachers' perceptions and could be the subject of further study.

Online communities

The online community section contained 12 open and closed questions designed to clarify the nature of the respondents' membership to the online community and their motivation for joining. It sought primarily to determine if an online community is perceived by its members as a medium for professional development. Half of the questions were open and this was purposefully constructed so that the emphasis was more on eliciting personal opinions rather than answering questions that led the respondents in a particular direction. As with the previous section on professional development, responses regarding online communities will be presented in the following subsections relating to each of the relevant survey items.

Community membership

To develop a better understanding of the circumstances of the respondents' membership behaviour, they were asked to indicate how many online communities they were a member. These were not distinguished between professional or personal interest communities and it was hoped that the actions of the respondents would be understood more clearly. The results can be seen in Table 4.10. .

Table 4.10

Number of subscriptions to online communities (in descending order)

Number of community subscriptions	Number (%) (*N*=98)
1 to 3	55 (56.12%)
4 to 6	22 (22.45%)
7 to 10	10 (10.2%)
Just this one	9 (9.18%)
10	2 (2.04%)

The largest response indicated that the majority of respondents were members of 1 to 3 online communities (56.12%). Although outside of the scope of the survey, it would be interesting to examine if these communities were all professional communities and if they were highly organised or casual groups. It could then be conjectured that the respondents may represent a group that uses this form of community in all aspects of their life not just for their professional needs.

Being a member of 1 to 3 online communities would not be regarded as difficult to manage in terms of time however, belonging to more than 3 would be seen as a significant number of subscriptions to manage. This time management would similarly be expected from the second largest grouping where respondents indicated that they were members of 4 to 6 online communities (22.45%). This may suggest that they, along with those respondents who belonged to 7 to 10 groups (10.2%) and over 10 groups (2.04%), were members of a combination of both personal and professional communities. Thus it might be conjectured that 34.69% of respondents are potentially using online communities in all aspects of their life not just for professional interests.

It would have been useful to determine which type of community they first joined, that is, if they joined personal interest communities and experienced the potential of these communities

75

and then sought to apply this to their professional life or vice versa. The question that then emerges is the relationship between these two types of communities on members' perceptions of the value of such membership as opposed to the members who are only participating on one type of online community. There may not be any correlation between these two aspects and multiple memberships may be evidence of more confident and experienced members of the community applying their new skills to other aspects of their life. This might suggest that the low number of respondents who belong to only one community (9.18%) may represent the legitimate peripheral participants of their community. These respondents may be participating in the survey whilst being new to this kind of experience. They may represent a group trialling online communities or exploring their potential.

In order to establish if there was a correlation between the number of online communities the respondents were members of and the number of years teaching experience they had, these attributes were cross-tabulated. The results can be seen in Table 4.11.

Table 4.11

*No. of years teaching experience *Number of online community memberships*

		Number of online community memberships					Total (N=98)
		Just this one	1-3	4-6	7-10	10+	
No. of years teaching experience	1-5	1	5	3	1	0	10
	6-10	0	5	3	0	0	8
	11-15	0	8	2	2	0	12
	16-20	1	6	2	0	0	9
	20+	7	31	12	7	2	59

The results of the Pearson chi-square analysis of Table 4.11 revealed that there was a good probability of a significant relationship between these two variables: Pearson χ^2 (1, $N = 98$) = 8.083, $p < 0.946$. This score indicates that an influence exists between the numbers of years of

76

teaching experience being related to the number of online community memberships. If we examine the data in Table 4.10, we can see that the highest number of memberships to online communities can be found in the teachers who have over 20 years experience. If this is combined with the results depicted in Figure 4.1, then we can conclude that those members fall between the 40-49 and 50-59 age brackets.

Duration of membership

There were three online communities participating in the study (see Table 4.1) and the respondents were asked how long they had been a member of the community through which they had accepted the invitation to participate in the survey. The intention here was to determine a level of commitment through length of membership. The results are summarised in Table 4.12.

Table 4.12

Length of community membership

Length of community subscriptions	Number (%) (n=98)
Less than 1 year	15 (15.31%)
1-3 years	34 (34.69%)
4-6 years	34 (34.69%)
7-10 years	10 (10.2%)
10 + years	4 (4.08%)

The predominant responses were 1–3 years and 4-6 years (each returning 34.69% of all responses). The outlying findings were from those who belonged to the online community for longer than 6 years (14.28%) and those who had been a member for less than 1 year (15.31%). As noted in the discussion on the number of subscriptions held, membership to a community requires a commitment of time and energy hence if members did not feel such membership was worthwhile, that is, able to satisfy their needs, it would be expected that they would "drop off" fairly quickly.

A self-evident factor which affects the length of membership time is the length of time the online community has existed. At time of writing, the Oz-TeacherNet community has been in operation for 11 years (since 1995), BECTA TopTeachers 4 years (since 2002) and SSABSA English Teachers for 3 years (2003) (see Table 4.1). This explains the finding that the majority of respondents' period of membership fell between 1-6 years. As can be seen in Table 4.12, 14.28%

of respondents had moved past this stage and thus represent a committed membership cohort from the Oz-TeacherNet list whose needs, it can be cautiously conjectured, are being met by this online community.

A further factor becomes apparent when the respondents who have been members for over 10 years are considered separately. This group, potentially 4.08% of the respondents, represents a cohort of early adopters of Internet-based communication as the Internet in its current form has existed and been easily accessible since 1995. The subset of this cohort (4.08%) who have been members of an online community for over 10 years would most probably also have been members of *Keylink* communities which had a radically different interface from what is now used and a different membership profile. It may indicate that this cohort includes teachers who have consistently embraced new developments in online communications. Specifically in online communications and more generally in ICT applications.

In order to understand if there was a relationship between the number of online communities the respondents belonged to and the number of years they have been a member of these communities, these two variables were cross tabulated using Pearson chi square. This process generated interesting statistics regarding membership over a period of time. The respondents who belonged to 1-3 communities and had been a member for 1-3 years represented 25.51% of the sample but this figure iteratively halved as the number of years increased 4-6 years (13.26%), 7-10 years (5.10%) and 10+ years (2.04%). This may indicate that there is a period of intensity for membership (1-3 years) and that membership naturally diminishes over time. It would be interesting to examine if members felt there were any differences in the level of their participation between professional, personal interest, formal or informal communities. The results of the Pearson chi-square analysis of these two variables (number of online communities belonged to and duration of membership) revealed that there was no explicit relationship between these two variables: Pearson χ^2 (1, $N = 98$) = 18.566, $p < 0.100$. So it might be conjectured that the number of communities an individual belongs to does not affect their length of time as a member. Conversely, people who have been members of online communities for a longer period of time need not expand their membership to a number of lists.

Selecting community membership

In an attempt to understand how the online communities attract members, respondents were asked how they found their particular online community. These results can be seen in Table 4.13.

Table 4.13

Information source for online community (in descending order of response)

Information source	Number (%) (N=98)
Link from a professional website	40 (40.82%)
Recommendation from a friend/colleague	32 (32.65%)
Other	12 (12.24%)
Requirement for further study, for example, postgraduate course	9 (9.18%)
Search engine	5 (5.1%)

Due to the nature of professional online communities, it would be expected that the respondents would have heard about these communities via professional means. This expectation is grounded here through the discovery that 32.65% found the community via a recommendation from a friend or colleague and 40.82% found it via a link from a professional website. Thus the majority (73.47%) joined the community via professional "introductions" which is indicative of a high sense of professional responsibility. A noteworthy group (9.18%) had joined the online community as a requirement for further study such as a postgraduate course. While some respondents may still be students in their courses, it is anecdotally known that many individuals retain membership following completion of their studies.

The respondents who contributed to "Other" (12.24%) clarified this choice as being (a) a requirement for their job, (b) via a forwarded email, (c) from a conference presentation, (d) via snail-mail, and (e) via an invitation from the community itself. Very few respondents (5.1%) located their community via a search engine and perhaps this group represented a cohort who are highly independent or who feel isolated in their workplace. They have actively and deliberately sought a specific group to join.

Time allocated to participation

The respondents were asked to estimate the number of hours they spent per week participating in the online community. Cues were given through the listing of specific online activities, that is, reading emails, replying to discussion threads or other activities on the website. The results can be seen in Table 4.14.

Table 4.14

Average time online per week (in increasing time allocation)

Information source	Number (%) (N=98)
Less than 1 hour	22 (22.45%)
1-3 hours	37 (37.76%)
4-6 hours	25 (25.51%)
7-10 hours	6 (6.12%)
10+ hours	7 (7.14%)

The majority spent between 0-6 hours per week (85.71%) and this can be broken down to (a) less than an hour per week (22.45%), (b) 1-3 hours (37.76%), and (c) 4-6 hours (25.51%). The majority of respondents reported spending between 1-3 hours per week which does not represent a large commitment of their time. If this, however, was averaged to 1.5 hours per week it would represent a potential of 60 hours of PD per calendar year. Considering that the teachers involved in these online communities join voluntarily, it would indicate that they place a high value and worth on this participation.

Two variables warranted a closer examination, that is, the number of online communities the respondents belonged to and the average amount of time spent participating in the community per week. These two variables were cross tabulated using Pearson chi-square and can be seen in Table 4.15. The results of the analysis revealed that there was a small probability of a significant relationship between these two variables: Pearson χ^2 (1, N = 98) = 33.523, p < 0.030.

Table 4.15

*The number of online communities belong to *average time spent per week*

No. of Community memberships	Average time spent per week						
	0	> 1hr	1-3 hrs	4-6 hrs	7-10hrs	10+hrs	Total
" this 1"	0	3	2	3	0	1	9
1-3	1	12	29	7	2	3	55
4-6	0	5	5	7	3	2	22
7-10	0	1	1	7	0	1	10
10+	0	0	0	1	1	0	2
Total	1	22	37	25	6	7	98

This score does not support the conclusion that a connection exists between the number of online communities an individual may belong to and the amount of time spent per week participating in the online community. An individual may belong to only 1 community but may spend 10+ on activities associated with their selected community or communities where another individual may belong to 4-6 communities and spend only 1-3 hours per week in total on community-related activities. What seems apparent is that this covariance is dependent upon the individual and their level of engagement with that community.

Reasons for membership

The respondents were asked why they maintained their membership to the online community. The answers collected for this question were initially sorted into two broad groupings according to subject matter. These were answers that pertained to professional requirements, and those associated with emotional support.

The answers grouped in the professional requirements category were further divided into classroom/student needs and PD needs. Respondents whose answers fit in the classroom/students needs grouping commonly cited reasons such as access to subject-specific resources, handy hints for the classroom, new relevant content, access to expertise to solve classroom problems, sharing lesson ideas and support for classroom problems. These answers correlate to the aims of PD previously identified.

It can be confidently contended that individuals saw the online community fulfilling a PD role as this was a popularly-cited reason why they maintained their membership. This was further clarified as the opportunity to learn from other teachers/peers, access to like-minded professionals, professional discussions, opportunities to develop own teaching practices, sharing professional knowledge, "keep up with current professional trends," and a desire to be "professional in my role." Associated to this desire for professionalism was the capacity online community membership had to remove geographical limitations with some respondents suggesting it was one of the only ways teachers in remote locations could maintain their professional learning. Given the intent of the study described in this book was to investigate the role of online communities as professional development for teachers and given that the PD function of online communities has emerged voluntarily from the survey respondents, this is a critical finding.

The second grouping of answers to this item were associated with the emotional support of the teachers. These included such affective outcomes as enjoying input from other teachers, passing on information, the ability to ask for help, the collegial support, the warm environment, the professional stimulation, "the safety-net – there if needed," a sense of belonging and camaraderie. This emotional support, whilst appearing to be professionally-based has been identified by research (ACOT, 1996, p. 15) as being an important element in successful PD programs for teachers.

Expectations of membership

The respondents were asked if membership had met their expectations. This was overwhelmingly answered in the positive with 92.85% agreeing that their expectations had been met. This score might be explained by the survey respondents not being truly representative of their communities with (a) the more negative members not having responded to the request to participate in the survey, and (b) those whose needs were not being met having discontinued their membership.

Some of the positive responses to membership expectations included (a) it had exceeded expectations, (b) it has "increased my knowledge of other teaching practices," and (c) "there is such freedom in discussion." Some of the more critical responses pertaining to other members behaviour included the following verbatim suggestions:

(a)   suggesting that some members dominate;

(b)   suggesting that discussions can be general and random at times;

(c)   commenting that some requests seem trivial;

(d)   desiring some members to be less patronising;

(e)   indicating they would have liked more advice on careers; and

(f)   complaining that some flower their comments with too much theoretical 'garbage'.

These observations from members', particularly those concerned with other members' behaviours suggests there is a possible role for moderators within these communities.

Only two respondents returned definitively negative responses with one simply stating "no" and the other offering that "it's not really PD, rather just people searching for partner texts." This latter comment was from a member of the SSABSA community list, the English Teacher community, whose discussion had, for the month at the beginning of the school year, been dominated by teachers requesting suggestions for partnering texts [pairing up two texts for comparing and contrasting purposes] for their students. Upon further examination after re-visiting the archives and informally assessing the same month for three years, this appears to happen every year at that time. Perhaps the respondent had not been a member for long or was seeking different information from their community.

The one respondent who had simply answered "No" to this question was examined more closely. He had the following profile:

- Male
- Aged 50-59 years
- Primary school teacher
- 16-20 years teaching experience
- Professionally competent in IT
- PD quota of 37.5 hours per year
- Member of 1-3 online communities
- Member of online community for 7-10 years.
- Reason for membership given as being "interest, challenge, looking for new ideas"

These factors would indicate that being a long-time member of online communities might, in fact, have played a pivotal role in this respondent's professional development. Hence his simple negative response to whether membership has met your expectations appears contradictory. It might be a comment on the content of the list through which he had been invited to take part in the survey or might be a comment on what he was *expecting* when he joined. His initial expectations may have been different but his needs must be being satisfied otherwise his membership would not have continued for so long. It might alternately be a problem of definition (as noted in previous discussions in this chapter) where the term "professional development" has the connotation of formal learning or activities determined by external agencies.

In response to being asked if membership to the online community had met their expectations 5% of respondents answered "Yes and No" or "sometimes." This was further clarified as being dependent on the topic being discussed, "that you can gain contacts and be exposed to different perspectives, but the quality of the learning needs to be more selective." A criticism from three out of the five respondents in this group was the negative effect of "dominators" (here meaning a member who takes over community discussions). Upon closer examination of the profiles of these three respondents, it was determined that they were all members of the same online community, hence this may be a problem that was prevalent in that particular online community.

Participation

The respondents were asked to select a statement from a given list that best described their participation in the online community. The findings from this item are summarised in Table 4.16.

Table 4.16

Perception of participation (in descending order)

Participation	Number (%) (*N*=98)
My participation depends on the topic being discussed by the list, I participate more if I am interested in the topic.	53 (54.08%)
My participation fluctuates; I go through periods of high participation to low participation according to outside pressures.	23 (23.47%)
My participation depends on my needs. If I need help or advice then I am active, otherwise I do not participate.	12 (12.24%)
My participation is not limited to my own needs, I try to participate in most discussions.	8 (8.16%)

This finding would indicate that participation is largely directed by the topic the community is discussing. Member activity fluctuates and this is generally dependent on outside pressure. It might also indicate that members are seeking personally relevant topics to participate in to motivate them to participate. Members do not feel the need to comment on all topics raised or respond to questions asked and only participate when they have a particular interest or expertise to share.

Online membership as professional development

The next question in the survey asked directly if participation in an online community could be regarded as a meaningful form of PD. The majority of respondents (86.73%) agreed that participation in an online community represent meaningful PD. Despite the acknowledged bias of the respondents to the survey, this is a key finding for the study described in this book because, as previously stated, the intent of the study was to investigate the role of online communities as professional development for teachers.

The agreement was further clarified by the respondents who attempted to explain their belief. These explanations were grouped under the following broad reasons using the respondents' verbatim comments. The comments were found to be supported in research literature and these are displayed in Table 4.17.

Table 4.17

Perceptions of membership as meaningful PD

Reasons provided by respondents supporting the idea that participation in an online community represented meaningful PD	As evidenced in research
It enabled networking	Huberman (2001)
It has an advantage of immediacy and relevancy	Richardson (1992)
It is convenient time wise	Garet et al. (2001)
There was a pooling of expertise	Sorge and Russell (2000)
There is a building of collective knowledge	Boyle et al. (2004)
It encouraged professional conversation	Sorge and Russell (2000)
It encouraged active learning	Guskey (2002)

There were also suggestions that to ensure the learning within the community is meaningful and professional, a community member should (a) "keep a diary of involvement as proof of and to chart proactive self-sourced PD"; and, (b) "that a community is only as good as its members, so move on if you feel there is nothing to be gained".

Thirteen respondents (13.26%) replied in the negative to the question of whether participation in an online community could be regarded as a meaningful form of PD with 2 (2.04%) declaring "No" without clarifying and 10 (10.20%) offering "not really because…" type answers. The reasons proffered were generally based on (a) the learning styles used online and their possible suitability for everyone, and (b) that meaningful learning depended largely on individual members. Several respondents commented on the need to be active, to not adopt the role of a lurker and that for those who participate, the benefits are high. Some negative responses dealt with the subject matter of the group such as (a) incomplete information, (b) information based on personal opinions, (c) issues not entirely applicable to teaching, (d) general discussions not in-depth discussion and (e) "more like common room gossip."

Change to teaching practice

The respondents were asked if they had changed any of their teaching practices as a result of participating in the online community. Whilst some respondents did not feel they had changed

85

their teaching practices, others felt they had been exposed to new ideas and resources which they had used in their classrooms. Seventy-seven percent of respondents answered positively to this question with many able to provide examples. It was interesting to note that all of the examples given (> 50) were all technology-based which could be an example of the mode of learning influencing the outcome. The types of examples given were how to use *PowerPoint*[*], webquests, a homework program, Blogging, Email Buddies, the Quizzard of Oz competition and the Ian Lillico Homework Grid.

The respondents who answered negatively to this question (21.42%) were responding in one of three ways. The responses were (a) "No" (14.28%), (b) "Not Yet" (3.06%), and (c) "No" with a clarification offered (4.08%). The responses of the latter grouping were not entirely negative and it may have been the wording of the question that influenced the answer they selected. They clarified their choice with explanations such as (a) "seen issues from a new perspective," (b) "learnt some great ideas which I have used, many of my practices have been reinforced," and (c) "have used some of the ideas and resources." Perhaps there is confusion over what constitutes a change to teaching practices as those who used new ideas or resources would meet this criteria as they have conducted a lesson using something new and more critically, something sourced from the community. It is self-evident to suggest that they would not have been able to do this if had they not been a member of the online community.

Advantages of participation in online communities

The respondents were asked if they could identify any advantages of participating in online communities as a form of PD. An overwhelming number of responses identified time as one of the key advantages. The ability to log on and participate according to their own schedule was a clear advantage and the asynchronous nature of the communities gave them time to think, reflect and compose answers. The following positive comments were commonly raised by the respondents (a) the freedom of being able to access the PD in their own time, (b) the convenience, (c) no time pressures or structures to follow, (d) that is was flexible according to what else was going on their life and (e) that it was internally motivated were also mentioned. Several respondents also commented on the cost effectiveness of this form of learning, and that it did not involve travel. This was also identified by geographically isolated teachers as being a clear advantage. The complexity of time as an element in professional development has been addressed by Lloyd and Cochrane (2006) and the findings in this survey would support this complexity.

Another advantage commented on by several respondents was the relevancy of the subject matter that it was linked closely to real life, was targeted to their needs and was authentic. This has been identified by research (Lloyd & Cochrane, 2006; Richardson, 1990) as an important characteristic for meaningful PD for teachers.

A further advantage identified was the immediacy of the learning in an environment where responses are fast, solutions are created quickly and topics can be discussed rapidly. Finally, the professional dialogue facilitated with peers outside of their workplace which ensured wider experience and helped create a sense of community was also cited as an advantage of participation.

Disadvantages of participation in online communities

In order to develop a complete picture of membership, the respondents were then asked if they could identify any disadvantages of participating in online communities as a form of PD. It was interesting to note, and further supporting the findings of Lloyd and Cochrane (2006) that one of the most popular advantages (time) was also listed as a disadvantage. In this instance, though, it would appear it was more of a time management issue in this context. A large number of the respondents commented that careful management of time is needed to sort through all the email from the lists. Several mentioned the negative impact of dominators, discussions getting side-tracked, misunderstandings and members pushing personal agendas. It was also suggested that passive members, lurkers or reluctant members might not benefit from this form of learning. One respondent mentioned the lack of personal interaction might mean that "you could feel lonely." A further problem raised was the inability to verify participation and this being potentially problematical when operating under a PD quota.

Memorable discussion threads

The final question in this section asked the respondents if any of the discussion threads they had read or participated in had been particularly memorable. Those who answered in the negative (14.28%) offered no clarification except for one respondent who stated that it was "only memorable if relevant to you and your situation at a particular time." This reiterates the findings from previous sections of the survey that the content of discussions needs to be authentic and contextual.

Of the 85.72% who responded in the affirmative some commented that the most memorable threads were remembered for the wrong reasons such as flaming or heated discussions. The threads that were highlighted as memorable were on the following topics: the future of education in Australia, the politics of teaching, creationism, philosophical topics, new technology, intelligent design, Mac vs. PC, standardised testing and the ethics involved, homework programs, reporting to parents and working conditions. These provide an insight into the issues that currently concern the teaching profession in general, considering that the respondents represent a cross section of ages, teaching background and nationalities.

Use of ICT

The final section of the survey concerned the use of ICT and contained only one open question. This section assumed that the respondents would have the requisite competency in ICTs to be active members in their online communities and, hence, the question was concerned with ascertaining how they had gained their skills. This would provide more depth and understanding of the demographical cohort participating in the research. This assumption appeared correct because as noted above, the majority of respondents (37.76%) self-rated themselves as professionally competent regarding their level of confidence in using ICTs.

The respondents were asked how they had acquired their ICT skills and the answers could be grouped into four categories. The first and most popular category (64.32% of respondents) declared that their ICT skills were either self-taught, obtained by "doing" or by trial and error. This indicated that they were a confident cohort who have a tendency to immerse themselves in a new subject and acquire skills when/as needed.

The second most popular method was via a university-based course (22.42%) with most being postgraduate, particularly Masters courses. Given the higher numbers of older respondents and the length of teaching experience it is unlikely that their skills were gained in initial or pre-service training. The remaining respondents (13.26%) learnt their skills either through workplace-based learning or mentoring or from their students.

Summary of Survey

The purpose of the online survey was to gather demographic data and provide insight into the professional development experiences, attitudes and skills of members of online communities. As noted the survey was comprised of 25 questions organised around four topics. These were (a) Background (b) Professional development, (c) Online communities, and (d) ICT use. For purposes of clarity and to parallel more detailed findings presented thus far in this chapter, the summary of the survey will be organised around these four topics.

(a) background

The questions in the background section of the survey were designed to collect broad demographical information about the members of the online community, namely age, gender, area/level of teaching, number of years experience and level of confidence with ICTs. The data collected (see Table 4.2) indicated that the majority of respondents were female (81.63%) and aged between 40-59 years (59.18%). They most typically came from a primary school background (32.65%) (see Table 4.3) and were very experienced teachers with the majority having over 20 years (60.2%) of teaching experience. In a self-assessment of their ICT skills, the majority were competent to professionally competent (90.08%).

(b) professional development

This section of the survey was designed to explore the professional development (PD) experiences of members and elicit personal opinions and suggestions regarding this topic. The majority of PD experiences for the respondents were best described as 'Conferences, workshops and courses'. Courses or training that were associated with technology received favourable comments. The PD programs that presented strategies that could be implemented in their classroom, that allowed them to participate and those that exposed them to new ideas were described as leaving a favourable impression on them. The majority of respondents were required to satisfy a certain number of hours of PD per year and this was generally not perceived as a negative constraint.

The respondents felt that teaching staff (87.75%) were the most suitable group to decide on the content and form of PD programs, however it was also suggested under the 'Other' option that a combination of all groups would also be desirable too. There was a clear preference for face-to-face PD programs (53.05%) (see Table 4.6), away from the workplace (70.41%) (see Table 4.7) and conducted over 2-3 months (40.82%) (see Table 4.8). When the respondents were asked to rank eight statements regarding the aims of PD, the majority selected 'Positive change to teaching practice' (34.69%) closely followed by 'An improvement in student learning' (33.67%) .

(c) online communities

This section of the survey was designed to clarify the nature of the respondents' membership to the online community and their motivation for joining. The majority of respondents were members of 1 to 3 online communities (56.12%) (see Table 4.9) and had been a member of those communities for either 1-3 years or 4-6 years (each returning 34.69%) (see Table 4.10). Most of the respondents selected or found their online community via a link from a professional website (40.82%) or by a recommendation from a friend or colleague (32.65%) (see Table 4.11). The amount of time they spent per week on participating in the online community typically ranged from 0-6 hours per week (85.71%) (see Table 4.12).

The majority of responses given to explain why they maintained their membership could be grouped under two broad headings, that is, professional needs (classroom/student needs or PD needs) and emotional needs. When asked if membership had met their expectations, an overwhelming 92.85% of respondents agreed. This result could be explained by the demographical

89

characteristics of the respondents, which concluded they represented a highly experienced teaching cohort with professional competency in ICT. When asked to select the statement that best describes their participation, the majority chose 'My participation depends on the topic being discussed by the list, I participate more if I am interested" (54.08%) (see Table 4.14).

The respondents agreed that participation in an online community represented meaningful PD (86.73%) and 77% felt that they had changed their teaching practices as a result of participating in the online community. The respondents were asked to identify any advantages of participating in online communities as a form of PD. An overwhelming number of responses identified time as one of the key advantages as well as the following positive comments were commonly mentioned (a) the freedom of being able to access the PD in their own time, (b) the convenience, (c) no time pressures or structures to follow, (d) that is was flexible according to what else was going on their life and (e) that it was internally motivated were also mentioned.

The respondents were also asked to comment on disadvantages and time management issues were commonly mentioned. Some also mentioned the negative impact of dominators, discussions getting side-tracked, misunderstandings and members pushing personal agendas. Finally, 85.72% of respondents agreed that discussion threads they had participated in or had read had been memorable and had made an impact on their pedagogy.

(d) ICT use

This section of the survey contained only one question which was concerned with how the respondents had gained their ICT skills. The majority of respondents described themselves as having been self-taught (64.32%) and acquiring their skills by 'doing' or by trial and error.

Thus the purpose of the online survey was to gather demographic data and provide insight into the professional development experiences, attitudes and skills of the members of the online communities involved in the study. This phase of the data collection has helped build a detailed profile of the senders and receivers of the electronic messages that are an important component of the online communities frequented by teaching professionals. The intent of this study was to investigate the possible role online communities in the PD of teachers, and this has been revealed voluntarily from the survey respondents. It emerged through the data that the respondents recognised their online community as fulfilling a PD role and it was identified as a key reason for maintaining their membership.

This result was further supported when the respondents were directly asked if participation in an online community could be regarded as a meaningful form of PD. The majority of respondents (86.73%) agreed thus indicating the potential role online communities may play in the PD of teachers. It was apparent that there exists some confusion regarding the definition of PD and what teachers perceive to be PD or not. When the respondents were asked to describe their PD experiences they listed both formal and informal self-directed programs as PD. However, when asked to comment on the form PD should take, such as location and duration they reverted to more traditional conceptions such as short programs in a neutral (away from workplace) environment. Thus indicating that comprehending online communities as a context for PD is currently not happening nor is it being perceived as a formal option for professional learning.

Perhaps a clearer indication of the value of online communities as a form of professional learning for teachers is more apparent when member behaviour is examined more closely. When the respondents were asked what kept them as a member of the online community the responses were broadly grouped under professional requirements and emotional support. The impact of their membership becomes clearer when examples of these two groupings are presented in Table 4.18.

Table 4.18

The impact of membership to online communities on members

Membership behaviour that meets professional requirements	Membership behaviour that meets emotional support
- the opportunity to learn from other teachers	- good to have reinforcement that problems are not mine only
- good source of quick help	
	- I enjoy the input from other teachers plus on the odd accession I can help someone
- access to a group of like-minded professionals	
	- the collegial support online from others in the country and internationally
- the wealth of knowledge available at the drop of a hat	
	- friendships
- the content is often relevant to my work	
	- safety-net – there if needed
- on-going interest in what is happening in other geographical areas	
	- sense of belonging and a common goal
- keeping up-to-date with trends and general developments in teaching/learning	- camaraderie, we are all in this together trying to make things work
	- no more isolation

The responses listed in Table 4.18 clearly indicate that members' needs are being successfully met and there is anecdotal evidence that members are engaging in professional learning. Thus the survey has provided rich demographical data that has helped present a clearer picture of the members of online communities and their perceptions regarding the value and worth of such membership within the context of PD. This has helped create a sense of who is sending and receiving the electronic messages within the community and helps to develop some understanding of the impact of those messages on members.

5. Findings: Community Transcripts

The expertise and knowledge on a subject or topic available to a teacher or teacher network is only limited by the number of online contacts

(Hawkes, 1999, p.47)

Overview

The previous chapter, which presented findings from the electronic survey, began with a statement, expressed as a simple equation, about electronic communication and how it is characteristically concerned with "the message" (eM), those who send them (S) and those who receive them (R). This chapter will focus on the messages (eMs) sent and received by members of the three online communities investigated in this study during a selected calendar month (January, 2006).

This focus takes two distinct forms. The first is on analysing the content of the messages themselves in an attempt to discern *what* is being said. The messages were coded using the phases and descriptors of the Practical Inquiry Model described in Chapter 3. Messages were deemed to be (a) evocative, (b) inquisitive, (c) tentative, or (d) committed.

The second focus is on graphically mapping the actions and interactions of the community using *MAXMaps* software. This process investigates *how* the community interacts and is based on the premise that understanding the content of messages is not limited to the actual message itself. Electronic messages are sent either to initiate or respond to a discussion thread and examining the entry point of a new message can help to clarify the dynamics of the community discussion. This chapter will present a general overview of thread pattern analysis and will explore flowchart patterns, regular cluster patterns and bonded cluster patterns. It will conclude with a summary of the findings from the community discussion transcripts.

Community discussion transcripts

In any investigation of an online community, what is said is of critical importance. The simple act of counting messages is only a partial measure of the success and reach of the community. More complex measures of community impact can only be drawn from the analysis of the messages themselves. It was decided that the community transcripts would be selected from the same time period for each of the three communities (see Table 5.2) and January 2006 was randomly chosen. It was hoped that, as this represented the start of a new school year in Australia, and the end of Term 1 in the United Kingdom, there would be rich data to analyse. Table 5.2 repeats relevant data from Table 4.1 and adds the number of messages coded in this study.

Table 5.2

Teacher online communities activity (January 2006)

Community Name	Acronym	Membership (as at January, 2006) ($N=1288$)	January 2006 Messages ($N=546$)
BECTA Top Teachers	BECTA	568	176
Oz-TeacherNet	OTN	608	333
SSABSA – English Teachers	SSABSA	112	37

Clearly the first two online communities, BECTA Top Teachers and Oz-teachers present as more active and vibrant communities than the smaller discipline-specific SSABSA community. As reported above, the 333 messages in the Oz-TeacherNet transcript were not from 333 unique senders but from 20-30% of their total membership base of 608.

As mentioned in Chapter 3, the item of analysis was the message itself. As Henri (1990) suggested, each message has its own meaning and can be considered on its own (p. 118). A message posted during an online discussion or posted to a noticeboard in response to a discussion thread is generally limited to one topic. However, it became difficult to code some messages as they addressed several points or messages. In an effort to solve this problem, the message was coded according to the first data that was presented in the message, for example, if the message began with a T2 (see Table 4.17 for an explanation of the coding) message and then moved to E1, it was coded as T2. The rationale was that the primacy or urgency of the first-addressed topic would be indicated by the writer's making this the leading sentences of the message. This served as a workable compromise but was not wholly satisfactory as it was felt some valuable data was not able to be acknowledged or used due to the limitations of the unit of analysis. The limitations that emerged during the coding phase will be discussed further in Chapter 7.

Whilst the community transcripts were accessed through public archives they required a member username and password to access. Messages were coded and analysed using the Practical Inquiry Model (Garrison et al., 2001) which attempts to recognise and incorporate both the shared world and the private world of an individual as argued to be important components in the construction of knowledge. This model's strength is its applicability to online Communities of Practice due to the shared/private world perspective. This aspect can be seen in the diagram of the model Figure 5.1.

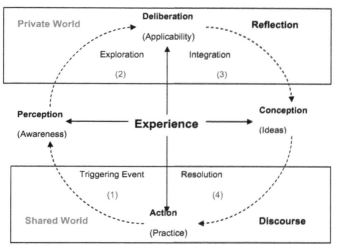

Figure 5.1: Practical Inquiry Model (Garrison et al., 2001)

General Overview of codes

Messages are classified according to the four phases of the model which are (1) triggering event, (2) exploration, (3) integration, and (4) resolution. These four phases reflect the critical thinking process and indicates a cognitive presence (Garrison et al., 2001). In this study, the phases will be combined with four broad descriptors; (a) *evocative*, (b) *inquisitive*, (c) *tentative* and (d) *committed* (Figure 5.1 further clarifies this relationship). The coding scheme to be used will reflect these descriptors, for example, the "evocative" descriptors will be referred to as E1 and E2. An overview of the coding of the three community transcripts for January 2006 is presented in Table 5.3.

Table 5.3

Overview of coding: BECTA, OzTeachers and SSABSA Transcripts (January 2006)

Message phases and descriptors (codes)		# of messages per phase	% of messages per phase
		(N=546)	
EVOCATIVE CODES	(Triggering event)	101	18.5%
INQUISITIVE CODES	(Exploration phase)	121	22.16%
TENTATIVE CODES	(Integration phase)	270	49.45%
COMMITTED CODES	(Resolution phase)	54	9.89%

From Table 5.3, it can be seen that the messages posted fitted all four phases and indicators from the Practical Inquiry Model (Garrison et al., 2001). Table 5.3 shows that there were 101 evocative (triggering event) messages (18.5% of all messages sent), 121 inquisitive (exploration) messages (22.16%), 270 tentative (integration) messages (49.45%), and 54 committed (resolution) messages (9.89%). The composition of these messages as percentages of the total number of messages posted (N=546) is represented in Figure 5.2.

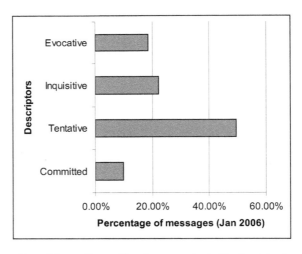

Figure 5.2   Composition of messages (sorted by descriptors)

The discussion in this section will now focus on providing and illustrating explanations of the code descriptors, namely, evocative, inquisitive, tentative, and committed. Following this will be a discussion of the transcripts by community, that is, BECTA Top Teachers, Oz-TeacherNet, and SSABSA English Teachers.

Evocative (Triggering Event)

As noted, the total number of messages in this phase was 101, which represent 18.5% of the total (*N=546*). This ratio would be expected as these types of messages are merely the trigger for the community discussion and their purpose is to inspire or provoke further debate and discussion. "Evocative" messages can be divided between E1 *Recognising the problem* and E2 *Sense of puzzlement* codes. The breakdown between E1 and E2 messages is shown in Table 5.4.

Table 5.4

Evocative messages: BECTA, OzTeachers and SSABSA Transcripts (January 2006)

Message phases and descriptors (codes)	# of messages per phase (*N=546*)	# and % of messages per descriptor
EVOCATIVE CODES (Triggering event)	101	
E1 Recognising the problem		37 (36.63%)
E2 Sense of puzzlement		64 (63.37%)

In the analysis of messages from the three communities in January 2006, there were 37 E1 messages (36.63%) and 64 E2 messages (63.37%). Typically E1: *Recognising the problem* messages contained requests supported by contextual information to help members understand what is required. For example:

> I've just been having a look at Google Earth – looks fantastic! I was wondering if anyone has come up with any good classroom uses for it - it looks like it would be great for exploring Roman Roads for example.

> BECTA Transcript Lines: 6162-6165

E2: *Sense of puzzlement* messages tended to be about professional issues or topics not directly related to a specific classroom problem, for example:

> As a secondary maths teacher, from time to time I encounter the question "When am I ever going to use this?" What's the point of learning algebra or trigonometry? The

implication of the question is that the study of these branches of mathematics is pointless because few people will ever need to put them to use in their chosen career. How do we answer such questions?

Actually, it's a fair observation that most people will not need to use many of the skills we teach in secondary school. Apart from specific skills that are taught on the job, almost all the knowledge and skills needed by the vast majority of occupations have been taught by about year 5. I'm not just talking about maths ... the same thing goes for the other learning areas. So what do *you* say when they ask you, "When am I ever going to use this?"

OzTeacherNet Transcript Lines: 4504-4532

Inquisitive (Exploration)

The exploration phase is illustrated by six "inquisitive" descriptors (I1-I6). These are used to identify (a) divergence within the online community (Code I1), (b) divergence within a single message (Code I2), (c) information exchange (Code I3), (d) suggestion for consideration (Code I4), (e) brainstorming (Code I5), and (f) leaps to conclusions (Code I6). The breakdown of inquisitive messages is presented in Table 5.4

Inquisitive messages are posted in response to evocative (triggering event) messages (E1 and E2) but, in this instance, were more prolific in response to E1 messages. In this analysis, 121 inquisitive messages were identified representing 22.16% of all messages analysed (N=546). The breakdown of the coded inquisitive messages into the six descriptors can be seen in Table 5.5.

Table 5.5

Inquisitive messages: *BECTA, OzTeachers and SSABSA Transcripts (January 2006)*

	Message phases and descriptors (codes)	# of messages per phase (N=546)	# and % of messages per descriptor
	INQUISITIVE CODES (Exploration phase)	121	
I1	Divergence – within the online community		26 (21.49%)
I2	Divergence – within a single message		9 (7.44%)
I3	Information exchange		17 (14.05%)
I4	Suggestions for consideration		32 (26.45%)
I5	Brainstorming		15 12.4%)
I6	Leaps to conclusions		22 (18.18%)

The most frequently occurring message type was I4: *Suggestions for consideration* (n=32, representing 26.45% of all *inquisitive* messages). These were often messages that offered a solution to an E1 or E2 message but also included ideas or suggestions that warranted further exploration. These were commonly in the form of questions, for example:

> I would start with parents' views: from their experience of surfing, do they think it is possible to protect children from downloading unsuitable sites? And then, is it unsafe for children to make their own judgments about these sites?

BECTA Transcript Lines: 490-490

Inquisitive messages attempt to present a solution to a problem or question, but did not want to appear to be authoritative or dominating. The authors couch their suggestions with rhetorical questions that could be responded to by the community.

The second most frequently-occurring inquisitive messages were I1: *Divergence – within the online community* (n=26, representing 21.49% of all *inquisitive* messages). This did not indicate that arguments were rife among the communities just that differing opinions or ideas were being presented to be considered. An example of this is the following message concerning the use of interactive whiteboards:

> I'm wondering if anyone else is as doubtful as I am about the value of these? (The boards - I'm 100% in favour of projectors).
>
> I remain unconvinced that they offer anything that cannot be achieved by other means, other perhaps than for the youngest children where the touchy-feely thing is important (and where is the cut-off for this: Yr 2? 4?)

BECTA Transcript Lines: 2757-2762

The code, I6: *Leaps to conclusions* warrants some comment as it represents the dissonant voices within the community discussion. In this analysis, there were 22 I6 messages (representing 18.18% of all *inquisitive* messages). These types of messages may present as a natural occurrence within a discussion particularly among a diverse group of people. For example:

> If you're suggesting using it [the use of interactive whiteboards] in conjunction with handwriting recognition - be wary!

BECTA Transcript Lines: 3688-3689

I6 "leap to conclusions" messages tend to disagree with previous messages but do not offer any reason or explanation for the opinion offered. If a message disagreed with a previous message but offered supporting reasons or explanations, then it may have been coded as I1. I6 messages were the third most frequently occurring inquisitive messages.

The messages coded I3: *Information exchange* (*n*=17, representing 14.05% of all *inquisitive* messages) were mainly responses to E1 messages. They offered suggestions to a particular request and often contained hints or comments on their personal use of the idea. However, they could also be contributions such as finding new information and sharing it with the community. For example:

> I have a new word to share with everyone "confabulation". I'm doing research on the brain and came across this little beauty (well I thought it was anyway). We don't retain 100% of an elaborate experience as we store different aspects in different parts of the brain. Then when retrieving the information (as the brain abhors incompleteness) it may fabricate a missing or incomplete section. This is not lying because it is an unconscious process and the individual believes the fabricated information to be true.
>
> This is "confabulating". Certainly brings a different light on all those little confrontations between children when they swear that their version is true!!!! Are they lying or confabulating?????

> OzTeacherNet Transcript Lines: 8004-8013

Another commonly attributed inquisitive message was I5: *Brainstorming* messages (*n*=15, representing 12.4%). These messages were akin to brainstorming in face to face settings and building concepts maps within the discussion. Ideas, often many within one message, were offered for consideration. The following I5 example is also taken from the BECTA discussion on interactive whiteboards:

> Putting the pictures in the correct sequence is a perfect "drag'n'drop" activity. The use of the sound recorder allows the children to add a caption to each of the pictures.
>
> Alternatively the children could use the sound recorder on each page to build a simple play script. As each page is turned, a child records the characters' feelings by speaking the part.
>
> Using other hardware in conjunction with the board - an Alphasmart allows children to add text away from the board, but then just plug it into the host computer and the opportunity for discussion and engagement from peers is endless. Immediate access

to the board for everybody to see: "How could we improve on this?" "Which words could we add to this sentence to make it clearer?"

Tentative (Integration)

Tentative messages were the largest number of messages (*n*= 270, which represents 49.45% of the total number of messages posted). The breakdown for the four tentative codes is seen in Table 5.6.

Table 5.6

Tentative messages: BECTA, OzTeachers and SSABSA Transcripts (January 2006)

Message phases and descriptors (codes)	# of messages per phase (N=546)	# and % of messages per descriptor
TENTATIVE CODES (Integration phase)	270	
T1 Convergence – among group members		74 (27.41%)
T2 Convergence – within a single message		32 (11.85%)
T3 Connecting ideas, synthesis		62 (22.96%)
T4 Creating solutions		102 (37.78%)

The timeline of a discussion, as per the model being used, can be roughly described as being the presentation of a problem (evocative), the clarification and exploration of that problem (inquisitive), a possible solution being reached (tentative) and finally, the solution being implemented (committed). Therefore, we would expect that a large number of messages within the tentative phases would be concerned with creating solutions and connecting ideas. These types of messages offered specific solutions to a problem usually after the community had agreed on a course of action to follow.

The triggering event for tentative (integration) discussions was generally E2 messages. E1 messages that contained a problem or situation that was quickly dealt with by the community were generally limited to inquisitive codes as the response and then moved directly to the resolution phase. However, more complex issues or discussion moved from the inquisitive phase, where the issues were generally clarified in the tentative phase.

These longer more complex discussions contained a large number of *T1 Convergence – among group members* messages (n=74, representing 27.41% of all tentative messages). For example:

> Well said, ... [Name], having experience two universities, I particularly agree with your comments about them. I had thought that as uni fees increased, we would begin to see some bang for our buck, so to speak. But each year we seem to pay more, and get less. It's all about quantity (in terms of student numbers) rather than quality. I feel some pressure to resume the M Ed, from which I have taken a leave of absence, before fees go even higher and become prohibitive.
>
> As a relief teacher I wonder why I bother, but you have to keep the old brain employed somehow, and I also enjoy the intellectual stimulation. Plus it will give me something to do on my days off. At the same time, concerned that the course lacks relevance and that I should perhaps explore what PD is available to me.
>
> I would be interested in hearing from people who were happy with their university experience and which one they attended.
>
> OzTeacherNet Transcript Lines: 829-842

These types of messages would often refer to a previous message or member with whom the author wishes to align their opinions.

The most frequently-occurring message descriptor was T4 *Creating solutions* messages (*n*=102*)*. This was the most frequent message type in its phase (representing 37.78% of all tentative messages) as well as being the most frequent of all messages posted (representing 18.16% of all messages in January). T4 messages appeared to be "culmination" solutions reached after much discussion. For example;

> Getting students to do a comic sports commentary can be fun, or [be] a sports commentator interviewing a literary character (say Macbeth, do you think you kicked an own goal when you tried to get rid of Banquo? Ans: Yes I didn't think they'd bring on his ghost as a substitute) Kids often like satires, e.g. visiting crikey.com, or some such. Getting students to choose their own scene to dramatise from a film or novel can produce great results.
>
> SSABSA Transcript Lines: 66-72

The process of reaching this agreed course of action required many messages which were classified as T3*: Connecting ideas and synthesis* (*n*=62, representing 22.96% of all tentative messages). Generally, one member of the community attempted to tie together all of the other ideas or proposals. Often this member was the initiator of the evocative message (E1 or E2) that

102

had started the discussion. It could be seen as an attempt to move the discussion towards the next phase and resolving the issue being discussed. For example (a further message from the BECTA discussion on interactive whiteboards):

> One of the more subtle differences between both is the positioning of the teacher and the class. In my experience, generally the standard data projector is projected onto a wall at well above head height whereas the typical [interactive whiteboard] IWB installation by necessity has to be at the eye level of the children. (They and the teacher need to be able to reach the top of the board where the standard menus are.) Being usually a slightly smaller image "throw" the class can also sit closer to the board. With the IWB, the teacher is usually facing the class as opposed to working from the computer typically behind the class. This overall intimacy tends to draw more out of both the children and the teacher as facial and other mannerisms can be reacted to a lot easier.

> BECTA Transcript Lines: 4653-4663

Finally, the last code in this descriptor to be discussed in this section, T2: *Convergence – within a single message*, was attributed to 32 messages (representing 11.85% of all tentative messages). These types of messages were generally lengthy and were where the author attempted to perform several tasks, such as offering solutions, connecting ideas or agreeing with several members.

Committed (Resolution)

This phase was attributed to least number of messages (n=54, representing 9.8% of all messages). As it was the final phase of the discussion and often acted as a closure to the discussion, this finding is not surprising. As there had been 101 triggering messages, it might have been expected that there would be a similar number of committed messages. That there were a total of 54 messages in this descriptor which may indicate that some discussions were not resolved or solutions were not flagged to the community as having been chosen. Some problems or questions may have been resolved in conversations outside of the community list or some may have been so simple so as not to warrant a formal closure, for example, answers to direct questions. The breakdown for the committed messages is seen in Table 5.7.

Table 5.7

Committed messages: BECTA, OzTeachers and SSABSA Transcripts (January 2006)

Message phases and descriptors (codes)	# of messages per phase (N=546)	# and % of messages per descriptor
COMMITTED CODES (Resolution phase)	54	
C1 Vicarious application to real world		30 (55.56%)
C2 Testing solutions		12 (22.22%)
C3 Defending solutions		12 (22.22%)

The most common type of committed message was C1: *Vicarious application to the real world* (*n*=30, representing 55.56% of all *committed* messages). C1 messages attempted to show how the solutions or ideas the group had agreed on applied in real or authentic situations. For example:

> Building on [Name] Q Bear, something I've seen done is to have two or three stuffed toys going home. (More children get a turn this way) Keep them in cloth bags (library bags) and as well as a diary to fill out include fiction/nonfiction books, e.g. if you have a koala include two or three books about koalas that parents can read to the children or children can read to younger siblings.
>
> Something else that is lots of fun and can take care of your whole literature/language programme for a term is Walking Talking Text, developed in the NT for use with aboriginal children.
>
> Thanks to others who have made suggestions. I can hardly wait for school to start
>
> :)
>
> OzTeacherNet Transcript Lines: 5696-5711

The remaining codes for messages in this descriptor; C2: *Testing solutions* and C3: *Defending solutions* could be described as an additional phase of the discussion. Whilst the main point of the community discussion was to reach a consensus or conclusion on a professional issue, or to solve a pedagogical problem some messages were outside of this initial conclusion. The messages that were classified as *C2, Testing solutions* (*n*=12, representing 22.22% of all *committed* messages) and *C3 Defending solutions* (*n*=12, representing 22.22% of all *committed* messages) often appeared later on this discussion list and referred back to the solution or course of action the member had planned to take. These messages often shared with the community the results of a particular course of action or defended the course of action that was taken. For example:

> Both the children and I found it really frustrating!

Despite using the wireless mouse and keyboard, I found that the whole pace of the lessons slowed down-no-one could type as quickly as they could walk up to the board and click or write and the interactivity was gone-you can't quickly move objects on the board with the mouse-first you have to catch the object!

BECTA Transcript Lines: 3895-3897

This section has presented an overview, through descriptive statistics, of all messages analysed in this study. It has also introduced the codes (after Garrison et al., 2001) which have been used in this analysis and provided illustrations of their use. The following sections will review each of the communities in turn and provide more details on the professional discussions each hosted during the test period (January, 2006).

Community transcript - BECTA – Top teachers

As previously noted, the community transcript from BECTA – Top Teachers for January 2006 contained 176 messages which represents 32.23% of the total number of messages coded (N=546) (see Table 5.4). Although this online community had a total of 568 subscribed members, the number of active members would be estimated at being around 20-30% of that total.

Table 5.4

Total number of messages for BECTA – Top Teachers

Community Name	Acronym	Membership (as at January, 2006) (N=1288)	January 2006 Messages (N=546)
BECTA Top Teachers	BECTA	568	176

This online community is based in the United Kingdom and is concerned mainly with implementing and using ICTs in the classroom. It was interesting to read the types of innovations and ICTs that were commonly used and the types of issues that concerned this group of teachers. The overall results of the coding followed the trends that were highlighted in the general overview and can be seen in Table 5.3.

Table 5.5

Coding of transcript from BECTA Top-Teachers January 2006

Message phases and descriptors (codes)		# of messages per phase (*N*=176)	# and % of messages per descriptor
EVOCATIVE (Triggering event) (*N*=101)		26	
E1	Recognising the problem		21 (80.77%)
E2	Sense of puzzlement		5 (19.23%)
INQUISITIVE (Exploration) (*N*=121)		39	
I1	Divergence – within the online community		12 (30.77%)
I2	Divergence – within a single message		6 (15.38%)
I3	Information exchange		0 (0.00%)
I4	Suggestions for consideration		11 (28.21%)
I5	Brainstorming		3 (7.69%)
I6	Leaps to conclusions		7 (17.95%)
TENTATIVE (Integration) (*N*=270)		98	
T1	Convergence – among group members		31 (31.63%)
T2	Convergence – within a single message		5 (5.10%)
T3	Connecting ideas, synthesis		22 (22.45%)
T4	Creating solutions		40 (40.82%)
COMMITTED (Resolution) (*N*=54)		13	
C1	Vicarious application to real world		8 (61.54%)
C2	Testing solutions		4 (30.77%)
C3	Defending solutions		1 (7.69%)

Evocative (triggering events)

There were 26 messages coded according to this descriptor which represents 14.77% of the total of messages posted to the BECTA Top-Teachers list in January 2006 (*n*=176). This follows the overall trend (18.5%) when measured against the findings for all three lists under review. However, the proportion of E1 *Recognising the problem* messages (*n*=21, 80.77%) and E2 5 *Sense of puzzlement* messages (*n*=5, 19.23%) is diametrically different from the overall results where E1 messages (*n*=37, 36.63%) and E2 messages (*n*=64, 80.77%) have different weightings. It is of further interest, however, that the BECTA list generated 21 of the total of 37 E1 messages (56.76%) while generating only 5 of the total of 64 E2 messages (7.81%). Both findings are disproportionate for a list which has generated 32.23% of the total messages analysed (*n*=176, *N*=546). This may represent a difference in the use of the discussion list by members, as more of a problem solving forum.

Inquisitive (Exploration)

This descriptor was, as per overall trends, the second largest descriptor with a total of 39 messages which represents 22.16% of the total messages posted to the BECTA list in January 2006 ($N = 176$). However, the most common code differed between the combined results and that from the BECTA list. Table 5.6 shows the difference in order of frequency of the I1-I6 codes. While I5 and I6 have the same rank, that is, Rank 5 and 3 respectively, the other codes (I1-I4) differ.

Table 5.6

Comparison between combined transcripts and BECTA Top-Teachers (I1-6)

Code	Descriptor	Combined		BECTA	
		Rank	%	Rank	%
I1	Divergence – within the online community	2	21.49%	1	30.77%
I2	Divergence – within a single message	6	7.44%	4	15.38%
I3	Information exchange	4	14.05%	6	0.00%
I4	Suggestions for consideration	1	26.45%	2	28.21%
I5	Brainstorming	5	12.4%	5	7.69%
I6	Leaps to conclusions	3	18.18%	3	17.95%

This result might indicate that there is more debate and discussion present in this community perhaps as the result of dominators or strong personalities. Some comments collected from the survey indicated that this problem existed in this community. Of particular interest in the BECTA findings is for I3: *Information exchange* which was not attributed to any messages posted to this list.

Tentative (Integration)

This descriptor remained consistent with overall trends by representing the largest number of coded messages being 98 (55.68%) compared with the combined lists with 270 (49.45%) of all messages. It also followed the trend for coding particularly for T1: *Convergence among group members* (Combined: 27.41%; BECTA: 31.63%), T3: *Connecting ideas, synthesis* (Combined: 22.96%; BECTA: 22.45%) and T4: *Creating solutions* (Combined: 37.78%; BECTA: 40.82%). There was a marked difference on the T2: *Convergence within a single message* (Combined: 11.85%; BECTA: 5.1%). These were, however, the lowest measure in each instance.

Committed (Resolution)

As with the overall results, this descriptor scored the smallest number of messages overall being 13 (7.39%) compared with the combined lists with 54 (9.89%) of all messages. As with other measures, it largely followed overall trends with C1: *Vicarious application to the real world* being the most frequently-attributed code (Combined, $n=30$, 55.55%; BECTA, $n=8$, 61.54%) recording the largest number of messages. However, it did differ with the remaining codes. The recorded findings for C2: *Testing solutions* (Combined, $n=12$, 22.22%; BECTA, $n=4$, 30.77%) and C3: *Defending solutions* (Combined, $n=12$, 22.22%; BECTA, $n=1$, 7.69%). This shows an emphasis on C2 that was not present in the overall trends and may indicate a difference in the dynamics or behaviour of the online community.

Community transcript – Oz-TeacherNet

The community transcript from OzTeacherNet contained 333 messages which represents 60.99% of the total number of messages coded ($N=546$) and by far the largest grouping in this study (see Table 5.7).

Table 5.7

Total number of messages for OzTeacherNet

Community Name	Acronym	Membership (as at January, 2006) ($N=1288$)	January 2006 Messages ($N=546$)
Oz-TeacherNet	OTN	608	333

As previously noted, this online community had a total of 608 subscribed members but the number of active members would be estimated at being around 10-20% of that total. This online community is based at the Queensland University of Technology (QUT), in Brisbane, Australia and is concerned mainly with pedagogical and professional issues affecting teachers. The results of the oz-TeacherNet coding presented in Table 5.8 closely followed the overall trends highlighted in Table 5.3.

Table 5.8

Coding of transcript from oz January 2006

Message phases and descriptors (codes)	# of messages per phase (*N*=333)	# and % of messages per descriptor
EVOCATIVE (Triggering event) (*N*=101)	71	
E1　Recognising the problem		14 (19.72%
E2　Sense of puzzlement		57 (80.28%)
INQUISITIVE (Exploration) (*N*=121)	72	
I1　Divergence – within the online community		13 (18.06%)
I2　Divergence – within a single message		3 (4.17%)
I3　Information exchange		15 (20.83%)
I4　Suggestions for consideration		18 (25.00%)
I5　Brainstorming		10 (13.89%)
I6　Leaps to conclusions		13 (18.06%)
TENTATIVE (Integration) (*N*=270)	153	
T1　Convergence – among group members		41 (26.80%)
T2　Convergence – within a single message		27 (17.65%)
T3　Connecting ideas, synthesis		37 (24.18%)
T4　Creating solutions		48 (31.37%)
COMMITTED (Resolution) (*N*=54)	37	
C1　Vicarious application to real world		20 (54.05%)
C2　Testing solutions		7 (18.92%)
C3　Defending solutions		10 (27.03%)

Evocative (triggering events)

There were 71 messages coded according to this phase which represents 21.32% of the total of messages posted to the Oz-TeacherNet list in January, 2006. This compares closely with the overall frequency of 18.5%. The proportion of E1 (19.72%) and E2 (80.28%) messages however differ from both the overall findings (E1: 36.63%; E2: 63.37%) and the findings for the BECTA list (E1: 80.77%; E2: 19.23%). There were, therefore, dramatically more *E2 Sense of puzzlement* codes than E1 and this may represent a difference in the use of the discussion list by members, that is, as more of an exploratory forum.

Inquisitive (exploration)

This phase was, as per overall trends, the second largest (of the four) with a total of 72 messages (21.62% of messages posted to the oz-TeacherNet in January 2006) compared with 121 messages (22.16% of all messages recorded by the three communities). The total number of oz-TeacherNet *inquisitive* messages (n = 72), however, equalled the number of *evocative* messages (n=71). This differs from the other two lists where, in each case, there are more inquisitive than evocative messages (BECTA: an increase of 150%; SSABSA: an increase of 250%; Combined: an increase of 119.8%). The most frequently-attributed code for this phase which was consistent with overall trends, I4 *Suggestions for consideration* (n=16, 25%). This was followed closely by *I3 Information exchange* (n=15, 20.83%). This result might indicate that there is less debate and more supportive discussions present in this community. The remaining codes scored as follows; I1 and I6. (n=13, 18.06%), I5 (n=10, 13.39%), and I2 (n=3, 4.17%). The latter result, *I2 Divergence – within a single message*, is very low but is, as with the highest rating in this phase, was consistent with the overall results.

Tentative (Integration)

This phase remained consistent with overall trends by representing the largest number of coded messages 153 *(N*=333, 45.95%) sent to the OzTeacherNet in January 2006. As previously noted, there were markedly more *tentative* messages overall (n=270, 49.45%) and sent through the BECTA list (*n=98,* 55.68%) than those attributed other descriptors. It also followed the overall trend for coding with the descriptors (in rank descending order) reporting the following: T4 (*n=48,* 31.37%), T1 (*n=41,* 26.8%), T3 (*n=37,* 24.18%), and T2 (*n=27,* 17.65%).

Committed (Resolution)

As with the overall results, this phase scored the smallest number of messages (*n=37,* 11.11%) posted to the oz-TeacherNet list in January 2006. It largely followed overall trends by reporting its largest number of messages as *C1 Vicarious application to the real world* (*n=20,* 54.05%). However, it did differ with the remaining codes, that is, C2: *Testing solutions* (*n=7,* 18.92%) and C3: *Defending solutions* (*n=98,* 55.68%) reporting a reversal of order from the BECTA list (C2 – 33.33%; C3 – 8.33%) and the SSABSA/Combined lists which gave equal weighting to C2 and C3. This emphasis on C3 may indicate a difference in the dynamics or behaviour of the online community.

Community transcript – SSABSA English Teachers

The community transcript from SSABSA – English Teachers contained 37 messages, which represents 6.78% of the total number of messages coded (*N*=546) and the smallest grouping in this study (see Table 5.9).

Table 5.9

Total number of messages for SSABSA English Teachers

Community Name	Acronym	Membership (as at January, 2006) (N=1288)	January 2006 Messages (N=546)
SSABSA – English Teachers	SSABSA	112	37

This online community had a total of 112 subscribed members, but the number of active members would be estimated at being around 10% of that total. This online community is based in Adelaide, South Australia and is concerned mainly with issues affecting English teachers. The overall results of the coding generally followed the trends that were highlighted in the general overview and can be seen in Table 5.10.

Table 5.10
Coding of transcript from SSABSA English Teachers

Message phases and descriptors (codes)	# of messages per phase (N=37)	# and % of messages per descriptor
EVOCATIVE (Triggering event) (N=101)	4	
E1 Recognising the problem		2 (50.00%)
E2 Sense of puzzlement		2 (50.00%)
INQUISITIVE (Exploration) (N=121)	10	
I1 Divergence – within the online community		1 (10.00%)
I2 Divergence – within a single message		0 (0.00%)
I3 Information exchange		2 (20.00%)
I4 Suggestions for consideration		3 (20.00%)
I5 Brainstorming		2 (20.00%)
I6 Leaps to conclusions		2 (20.00%)
TENTATIVE (Integration) (N=270)	19	
T1 Convergence – among group members		2 (10.53%)
T2 Convergence – within a single message		0 (0.00%)
T3 Connecting ideas, synthesis		3 (15.79%)
T4 Creating solutions		14 (73.68%)
COMMITTED (Resolution) (N=54)	4	
C1 Vicarious application to real world		2 (50.00%)
C2 Testing solutions		1 (25.00%)
C3 Defending solutions		1 (25.00%)

Evocative (triggering event)

There were only 4 messages coded according to this descriptor, which represents 10.81% of the total of messages posted to the SSABSA list in January 2006 ($N=37$). This falls short of the overall trend (18.5%) and the even split between E1 (50%) and E2 (50%) is not reflected in the findings from other lists and from the overall findings. The low number makes statistical comparisons difficult to sustain or to return valid data outside of noting general trends.

Inquisitive

This phase was, as per overall trends, the second largest descriptor with a total of 10 messages which represents 27.02% of the total number of messages posted to the SSABSA list in January 2006. While there was no reporting of the I2: *Divergence within a single message* descriptor, all other descriptors in this phase were represented. The most frequently attributed descriptor was I4: *Suggestions for consideration* ($n=3$, 30%).

Tentative (integration)

This phase remained consistent with overall trends by representing the largest number of coded messages ($n=19$, 51.35%) and reporting comparable weighting to other lists. The most frequently-occurring descriptor was *T4 Creating solutions* which was more heavily weighted than in other lists. However, T2: *Convergence within a single message* ($n=0$, 0%), was not identified and the second largest score was different to the overall trends, with *T3 Connecting ideas, synthesis* ($n=3$, 15.79%) scoring higher than T1: *Convergence among group members* ($n=2$, 10.53%).

Committed (Resolution)

As with the overall results, this phase scored the smallest number of messages ($n=4$, 10.81%). It largely followed overall trends by scoring the largest number of messages as *C1 Vicarious application to the real world* ($n=2$, 50%). The remaining codes were evenly distributed. This is fairly consistent with the overall trends.

Summary of community discussion transcripts

As mentioned previously, in any investigation of an online community, what is said is of critical importance and this chapter has addressed itself to understanding the content of the electronic messages collected from the three online communities involved in the study. It has been theorised that the communication equation is a relatively simple relationship of exchange between participants (see Chapter 4). But what has emerged from an analysis of the content of the messages is that this relationship may be more complex as it would appear to have influence and relevance outside the online environment. This analysis has helped to understand what is being said in the electronic messages and their effect on the members who interact with them.

Evidence of the complexity of the communication equation and its influence and relevance on members outside the online environment is clearly indicated by the content of the messages. The reference to members' private worlds (see Figure 5.1) in the form of offering shared experiences and possible solutions to problems are demonstrated by the messages coded Inquisitive and Tentative. The content of these messages clearly demonstrates the link between the shared world (the online community) and the private world (the members' workplace). This link presents as tangible proof of the influence and relevance of the communication equation outside the electronic environment.

The analysis of the content of the messages found in the transcripts was hoping to clarify what the members were looking for in their community and what their reasons were that led them to maintain their membership (see Table 5.1). It was hoped that the content of the messages would reveal if the members' professional requirements were being met and if the desired emotional support they sought was apparent. The messages should also provide confirmation that would support the reasons given by respondents as to why they remained members of their communities.

This complex measure of community impact can only be drawn from the analysis of the messages themselves and the transcripts from each community were collected for the month January 2006. The total number of messages coded per community can be seen in detail in Table 5.3. Two of the online communities, BECTA Top Teachers and Oz-teachers presented as more active and vibrant communities than the smaller discipline-specific SSABSA community, but it was estimated that the number of contributors for the month that was coded represented 20-30% of the total number of members per community. The unit of analysis was the message itself and the coding was completed according to the first data presented in the message.

An overview of the spread of messages per descriptor can be seen below in Table 5.11. Messages were classified according to the four phases of the Practical Inquiry Model (see Figure 5.2) which are (1) triggering event, (2) exploration, (3) integration, and (4) resolution. The phases were combined with four broad descriptors; (a) evocative, (b) inquisitive, (c) tentative and (d) committed (see Figure 5.2). The coding scheme used reflected these descriptors, for example, the "evocative" descriptors were referred to as E1 and E2. The total number of messages coded was 546 (*N*=546) and the number of messages per phase was; *Evocative* 101 messages (18.49%), *Inquisitive* 121 messages (22.16%), *Tentative* 270 messages (49.45%), and *Committed* 54 messages (9.89%) (see Table 5.3). Clearly the majority of messages were coded as Tentative.

113

This summary will be organized according to the data presented in this chapter, (a) community transcript – BECTA Top Teachers, (b) community transcript – OzTeacherNet and (c) community transcript – SSABSA English Teachers.

Table 5.11

Summary of the distribution of messages per descriptor (after Garrison et al., 2001)

	1	2	3	Total
Evocative (Triggering event)	26	71	4	101
Inquisitive (Exploration)	39	72	10	121
Tentative (Integration)	98	153	19	270
Committed (Resolution)	13	37	4	54
Total messages coded	176	333	37	546

Notes to Table 5.11

1. BECTA Top Teachers
2. Oz-TeacherNet
3. SS English Teachers

(a) Community Transcript – BECTA Top Teachers

The total number of messages coded was 176 (*n*=176) and the number of messages per phase was; *Evocative* 26 messages (14.77%), *Inquisitive* 39 messages (22.15%), *Tentative* 98 messages (55.68%), and *Committed* 13 messages (7.38%).

(b) Community Transcript – OzTeacherNet

The total number of messages coded was 333 (*n*=333) and the number of messages per phase was; *Evocative* 71 messages (21.32%), *Inquisitive* 72 messages (21.62%), *Tentative* 153 messages (45.94%), and *Committed* 37 messages (11.11%).

(c) Community Transcript – SSABSA English Teachers

The total number of messages coded was 37 (*n*=37) and the number of messages per phase was; *Evocative* 4 messages (10.81%), *Inquisitive* 10 messages (27.02%), *Tentative* 19 messages (51.35%), and *Committed* 4 messages (10.81%).

For each of the community transcripts, the majority of codes were in the descriptor *Tentative*. This would indicate that the communities are following the timeline of a discussion, as described previously. This can be described as the presentation of a problem (evocative), the clarification and exploration of that problem (inquisitive), a possible solution being reached (tentative) and finally, the solution being implemented (committed). Therefore, we would expect that a large number of messages within the tentative phases would be concerned with creating solutions and connecting ideas. These types of messages offered specific solutions to a problem usually after the community had agreed on a course of action to follow. This is summarised in Figure 5.3 below.

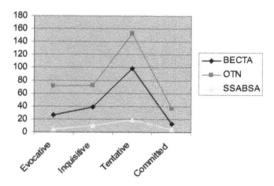

Figure 5.3 Summary of messages per descriptor per community

It was hoped that data would emerge from the analysis of the content of the messages that would provide tangible verification of what members were looking for in their community and their reasons for maintaining their membership. As can be seen in Table 5.12, there was a considerable number of messages that provided verification for each of the reasons identified by the respondents. Table 5.12 presents the number of messages supporting the reasons why the respondents sought membership to an online community. These were broadly grouped under the following two headings, professional requirements and emotional support. It can be concluded from this summary that membership to an online community does meet teachers professional requirements and does provide them with the emotional support they need.

Table 5.12

Verification of observable facts: professional requirements and emotional support

	What members are looking for in their community	Codes that provide verification of this observable fact	Number of messages per code
Professional requirements (a) classroom/student needs	- access to subject-specific resources	I3	17
		I4	32
		I5	15
		T3	62
		T4	102
	- new relevant content	I3	17
		I4	32
		T4	102
	- access to expertise to solve classroom problems	All Inquisitive and Tentative codes	391
	- sharing lesson ideas	I3	17
		I4	32
(b) PD needs	- learn from other teachers/peers	All Inquisitive and Tentative codes	391
	- professional discussions	All Inquisitive codes	121
	- opportunities to develop professional	All Tentative codes	270

	practices		
	- sharing professional knowledge	All Inquisitive and Tentative codes	391
Emotional support	- the ability to ask for help	All Evocative codes	101
	- a sense of belonging, camaraderie	All Inquisitive codes	121
	- collegial support	All Inquisitive codes	121
	- the 'safety-net' there if needed	All Evocative, Inquisitive and Tentative codes	492

It was also suggested that the data may provide evidence that would support the reasons given by the respondents for maintaining their membership. As can be seen below, Table 5.13 there is substantive number of codes supporting each of the reasons given by the respondents.

Table 5.13

Verification of observable facts: reasons for maintaining membership

Reasons for maintaining membership	Codes that provide verification of this observable fact	Number of messages per code
- great freedom in discussion and always supportive feedback	All Inquisitive codes	121
- increasing my knowledge of other teaching practices	All Inquisitive and Tentative codes	391
- provides practical and effective information	I3	17
	I4	32
	I5	15
	T3	62
	T4	102
- there is always someone available to guide, assist or give	All Evocative and Inquisitive codes	222

you advice on any given area		
- provides you with a group of peers to discuss ideas with	All Inquisitive codes	121

Thus two critical findings emerged voluntarily from the results of the survey and these would appear to be supported by evidence collected in the transcript analysis. The first was that the respondents recognised their online community as fulfilling a PD role and it was identified as a key reason for maintaining their membership. When the respondents were asked what kept them as a member of the online community the responses were broadly grouped under professional requirements and emotional support. After an analysis of the content of the messages, verifiable evidence has been found that supports these reasons (see Tables 5.12 and 5.13).

The second critical finding was when the respondents were directly asked if participation in an online community could be regarded as a meaningful form of PD. The majority of respondents (86.73%) agreed thus indicating the potential role online communities may play in the PD of teachers. The respondents provided several reasons to support that affirmation and when these are applied to those given for maintaining membership (see Table 5.14), there would appear to be supporting evidence from the transcript analysis to support this critical finding.

Table 5.14

Evidence of membership resulting in meaningful PD

Reasons for maintaining membership (taken from Table 5.12)	Codes that provide verification of this observable fact	Reasons provided by respondents supporting the idea that participation in an online community represented meaningful PD (taken from Table 4.17)
- great freedom in discussion and always supportive feedback - increasing my knowledge of other teaching practices - provides you with a group of peers to discuss ideas with	All Inquisitive codes and Tentative codes (391 coded messages)	- there was a pooling of expertise - there is a building of collective knowledge - it enabled networking - it encouraged professional conversation - it encouraged active learning
- there is always someone	All Evocative and Inquisitive	- it has an advantage of

available to guide, assist or give you advice on any given area	codes	immediacy and relevancy
	T3	- it is convenient time-wise
- provides practical and effective information	T4	
	(386 coded messages)	

The results from the data collected by the survey and community transcripts would appear to strongly support the two critical findings that emerged in Chapter 4. As can be seen in Table 5.12, online communities perform a professional development function for their members and Table 5.14 clearly shows that membership to such a community represents meaningful PD. It has also been demonstrated that the communication equation, $eM = S + R$, as mentioned in Chapter 4 has been shown to be more complex as it has the ability to transform participants, as evidenced by the messages illustrating their impact outside the online environment.

Thread pattern analysis

The coding of the three community transcripts provided rich data regarding the content and nature of the discussions that were taking place. It also provided evidence that a discussion has the potential to move through four distinct phases; evocative, inquisitive, tentative and committed. However, as has been previously suggested understanding the content of the messages is not limited to the actual message itself. An electronic message is sent either in response to or to start a discussion thread. Examining the entry point of a new message can help to clarify the dynamics of the community discussion.

The discussion threads were graphically mapped using *MAXMaps®* and these graphical representations help to develop a clearer understanding of the structure of electronic discussions. These have formed the basis of a thread pattern analysis and have been used to ascertain if there any standard patterns electronic discussions follow. These patterns may help to understand the differences between different discussion threads and the nature of those differences.

It is of interest to note that the communities, despite differences in size, location and purpose all evidenced the same patterns of message types. From the three community transcripts, nine discussion threads were followed. These threads were selected according to the criteria that they displayed the first three descriptors of the conversational analysis framework, that is, evocative, inquisitive and tentative. Of the nine identified thread patterns that were analysed, three distinct patterns emerged. These patterns emerged when graphical representations of the transcripts were developed. These patterns provided a wealth of information regarding the nature of online discussions. The patterns can be seen below in Figure 5.4. They are Pattern 1: *Flowchart design*, Pattern 2: *Regular cluster design* and Pattern 3: *Bonded cluster design*.

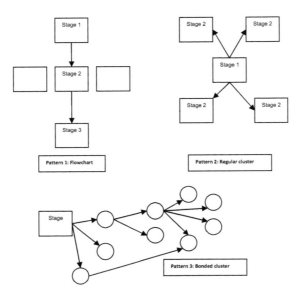

Figure 5.4 Flowchart Design Patterns

Pattern 1: Flowchart design

These discussion threads were simple and logical to follow and were conducted over an average period of time of 1-2 weeks. They were initiated by an evocative message (E1 or E2). Most commonly this type of message was a specific pedagogical problem with a clear context. The response from members of the community was immediately to offer tentative messages that is T4 *Creating solutions.* The initiator of the evocative message concluded the thread discussion by contributing a committed message indicating which suggestion they would adapt or use. This thread pattern has 3 clear evolutionary stages, which are:

Stage 1:   Evocative message (Triggering event) – the discussion is initiated by the posting of an E1 or E2 message.

120

Stage 2   Tentative (Integration) – attempts by the community to solve the problem develop over a period of 1-2 weeks with numerous contributors.

Stage 3   Committed (Resolution) – committed message from initiator indicating a solution has been found.

An example of this can be drawn from a discussion on the oz-TeacherNet list concerning homework for primary school students. This pattern has been mapped in Figure 5.5.

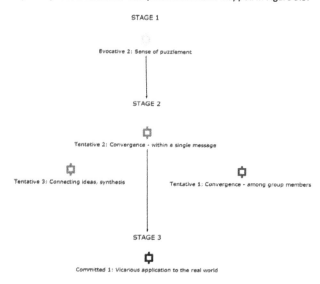

Figure 5.5 Example of flowchart design thread pattern

Pattern 2: Regular cluster design

Of the nine identified thread patterns that were analysed, three were classified as *Regular cluster design patterns*. These discussion threads were simple and conducted over a short period of time on average less than 1 week. These discussions are characterised by the following:

- They are initiated by an evocative message (E1 or E2).
- Generally a problem that has arisen which is usually explained within a context.
- The community then responds by offering tentative messages. In effect, they are brainstorming possible solutions (most typically I5 messages).

121

- The cluster does not have any resolution and there is no feedback from the initiator that they will try one of the suggestions.

This discussion has 2 evolutionary stages:

Stage 1:   Evocative message (Triggering event) – the discussion is initiated by the posting of an E1 or E2 message.

Stage 2   Tentative (Integration) – Brainstorming solutions / suggestions offered over a short period (approximately 1 week)

An example of this can be drawn from a discussion on the SSABSA list concerning group oral presentations for Year 11 students. This pattern has been mapped in Figure 5.6.

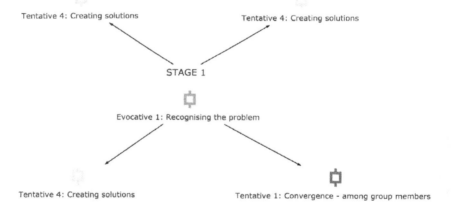

Figure 5.6 Example of regular cluster design thread pattern

Pattern 3: Bonded cluster design

Of the nine identified thread patterns that were analysed, two were classified as *Bonded cluster design* patterns. These were discussion threads that were more complex than mapped by the flow chart and regular cluster designs and were conducted over a longer period of time, that is, more than 2 weeks. These are characterised by the following.

122

- They are initiated by an evocative message (E1 or E2) but more typically an issue open for discussion (E2) rather than a specific problem that needs to be solved (E1).
- Often it was a topic or problem that requests personal opinions or thoughts to be shared with the community.
- The response to the evocative message maybe divided into two stages, namely inquisitive (exploration) and tentative (integration).
- The discussion progresses and switches between inquisitive and tentative stages multiple times.
- The discussion may be led in a new direction by a secondary evocative message.
- Throughout the stages of the discussion, some members may attempt to reach a consensus and offer committed messages to the community.
- The discussion does not end with a definite resolution and finishes in an inquisitive stage.

This discussion has multiple evolutionary stages. Stage 3, 4 or 5 can be partly present or repeated for an infinite number of times depending on the discussion:

Stage 1:   Evocative message (Triggering event) – the discussion is initiated by the posting of an E1 or E2 message.

Stage 2   Inquisitive &/or Tentative: Initial responses

Stage 3   Multiple manifestations of Inquisitive, Tentative and Committed messages

Stage 4   New Trigger: New evocative message associated to initial evocative message

Stage 5   Multiple manifestations of Inquisitive, Tentative and Committed messages.

Stage 6   Inquisitive: Conclusion, no resolution reached

An example of this can be drawn from a discussion on the BECTA Top Teachers list concerning the use of interactive whiteboards. Individual messages from this discussion were used in previous sections of this chapter particularly in categorising message types. This pattern has been mapped in Figure 5.7.

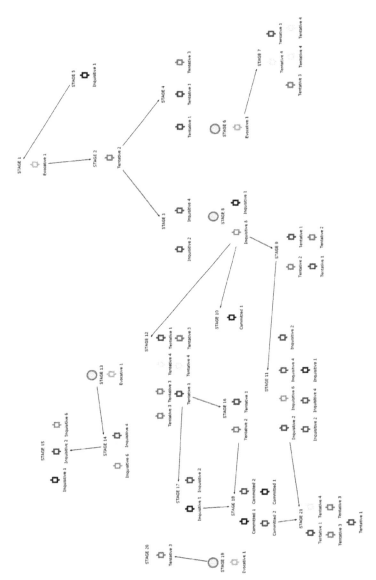

Figure 5.7   Example of bonded cluster design thread pattern

124

Summary of findings

(a) survey

The purpose of the online survey was to gather demographic data and provide insight into the professional development experiences, attitudes and skills of members of online communities. As noted in Chapter 4 the survey was comprised of 25 questions organised around four topics. These were (a) Background (b) Professional development, (c) Online communities, and (d) ICT use. A detailed picture of the members of online communities emerged (see Table 4.2) indicating that the majority were female (81.63%) and aged between 40-59 years (59.18%). They most typically came from a primary school background (32.65%) (see Table 4.3) and were very experienced teachers with the majority having over 20 years (60.2%) of teaching experience. In a self-assessment of their ICT skills, the majority were competent to professionally competent (90.08%).

With regard to the professional development (PD) experiences of members the majority of respondents described 'Conferences, workshops and courses' as their most typical experience. Programs that presented strategies that could be implemented in their classroom, that allowed them to participate and those that exposed them to new ideas were described as leaving a favourable impression on them. The majority of respondents were required to satisfy a certain number of hours of PD per year and this was generally not perceived as a negative constraint.

The respondents felt that teaching staff (87.75%) were the most suitable group to decide on the content and form of PD programs and there was a clear preference for face-to-face PD programs (53.05%) (see Table 4.6), away from the workplace (70.41%) (see Table 4.7) and conducted over 2-3 months (40.82%) (see Table 4.8). When the respondents were asked to rank eight statements regarding the aims of PD, the majority selected 'Positive change to teaching practice' (34.69%) closely followed by 'An improvement in student learning' (33.67%).

The majority of respondents were members of 1 to 3 online communities (56.12%) (see Table 4.9) and had been a member of those communities for either 1-3 years or 4-6 years (each returning 34.69%) (see Table 4.10). Most had found their online community via a link from a professional website (40.82%) or by a recommendation from a friend or colleague (32.65%) (see Table 4.11). They typically spent 0-6 hours per week on participating in the online community (85.71%) (see Table 4.12).

The majority of responses given to explain why they maintained their membership could be grouped under two broad headings, that is, professional needs (classroom/student needs or PD needs) and emotional needs. When asked if membership had met their expectations, an overwhelming 92.85% of respondents agreed however their participation was dependent on the topic being discussed by the community (54.08%) (see Table 4.14).

The respondents agreed that participation in an online community represented meaningful PD (86.73%) and 77% felt that they had changed their teaching practices as a result of participating in the online community. With regard to how they learnt their ICT skills the majority described themselves as having been self-taught (64.32%) and acquiring their skills by 'doing' or by trial and error.

Two critical findings emerged voluntarily through the results of the survey. The intent of this study was to investigate the possible role of online communities in the PD of teacher and it emerged through the data that the respondents recognised that their community fulfilled a PD role and this was identified as a key reason for maintaining their membership. The second critical finding emerged when respondents were asked if their online community could be regarded as a meaningful form of PD, 86.73% agreed. These two findings were further supported by evidence collected in the transcript analysis phase.

(b) community transcripts

The purpose of the community transcript analysis was to provide insight into the content of the electronic messages. It was hoped to clarify what the members were looking for in their community and what their reasons were that led them to maintain their membership (See Table 5.1). The total number of messages coded per community can be seen in detail in Table 5.3 and two of the online communities, BECTA Top Teachers (568 messages) and Oz-teachers (608 messages) presented as more active and vibrant communities than the smaller discipline-specific SSABSA community (112 messages) and it was estimated that the number of contributors for the month that was coded represented 20-30% of the total number of members per community.

An overview of the spread of messages per descriptor can be seen in Table 5.11. Messages were classified according to the four phases of the Practical Inquiry Model (see Figure 5.2) which are (1) triggering event, (2) exploration, (3) integration, and (4) resolution and these phases were combined with four broad descriptors; (a) evocative, (b) inquisitive, (c) tentative and (d) committed (see Figure 5.2). The total number of messages coded was 546 (N=546) and the number of messages per phase was; *Evocative* 101 messages (18.49%), *Inquisitive* 121 messages (22.16%), *Tentative* 270 messages (49.45%), and *Committed* 54 messages (9.89%) (see Table 5.3). The summary of the distribution per message, per community can be seen in Table 5.11.

The communities followed a timeline in their discussions, as described above. This was the presentation of a problem (evocative), the clarification and exploration of that problem (inquisitive), a possible solution being reached (tentative) and finally, the solution being implemented (committed). The largest number of messages were coded as tentative and were concerned with creating solutions and connecting ideas.

Data emerged from the content of the messages that provided tangible verification of the two key findings that emerged in the survey phase, that online communities perform a professional development function for their members and that membership to such a community represents meaningful PD. As can be seen in Table 5.12, there was a considerable number of messages that provided verification for the professional requirements and emotional support members were looking for from their community. These elements clearly demonstrate the online community performing a PD function. The content of the messages also provided evidence that supported the reasons given by the respondents for maintaining their membership. As seen in Table 5.14 there is a substantive number of codes supporting each of the reasons given by the respondents for maintaining membership which also demonstrated that it was meaningful PD.

(C) thread pattern analysis

The purpose of the thread pattern analysis was to ascertain if any electronic discussions follow specific patterns and if those patterns could help in the understanding of differences between electronic discussions and the nature of those differences. The coding of the three community transcripts provided rich data regarding the content and nature of the discussions that were taking place. However understanding the content of the messages is not limited to the actual message itself. An electronic message is sent either in response to or to start a discussion thread. Examining the entry point of a new message can help to clarify the dynamics of the community discussion.

Nine discussion threads were selected from the three online communities that displayed the first three descriptors of the conversational analysis framework, evocative, inquisitive and tentative codes. Of the nine thread patterns analysed, three distinct patterns transpired. These patterns were revealed when graphical representations of the transcripts were developed. These patterns provided a wealth of information regarding the nature of online discussions.

The flowchart patterns were straightforward and logical discussion threads. They were conducted over an average period of time of 1-2 weeks and were discussions that arose in response to a message with a specific (usually pedagogically-based) problem (example Figure 5.5). They were characterised as having three stages; trigger event, integration and resolution.

The regular cluster patterns were the simplest discussion threads, conducted over the shortest time-frame, usually less than one week. They followed an uncomplicated problem – solution pattern and once solutions had been offered, the discussion was concluded by the community (example Figure 5.6). They were characterised as having two stages; trigger event and integration.

The bonded cluster patterns were the most complex discussion threads, conducted over a longer period of time, usually more than two weeks. The thread was initiated by an evocative message, but the discussion may then be led in new directions or return back to original threads and did not have a definite resolution (example Figure 5.7). They were characterised as having six stages; trigger event and then multiple manifestations of messages and new triggers.

The three thread patterns that emerged provided a clearer understanding of the nature of discussion threads. It would appear that some discussion threads had a short period of sustainability (regular cluster threads) as communities dealt with problems or issues quickly. Some discussion threads followed a clear path of problem, solution and resolution as communities offered possible solutions to be considered and then one was clearly chosen to be applied (flowchart threads). The most common and most revealing thread pattern was the bonded cluster. This discussion thread clearly demonstrated the dynamic nature of electronic discussions as members responded to new triggers at different stages during the discussion. It also clearly showed the ability for asynchronous discussion to go back and re-visit previous messages and this non-linear capability would appear to be a unique feature of electronic discussions.

The sequence of data collection and analysis has been designed to inform and guide the direction of the study. The findings from the survey (Collection 1) identified issues or elements that needed further examination during the transcript analysis (Collection 2). These two data collections then informed the direction of the forum (Collection 3). This sequence of collection and analysis was designed to maintain clarity and integrity by re-visiting the research questions and propositions throughout this process. The results of the analysis will be presented in greater detail within the synthesis of findings in Chapter 6.

6. Synthesis of Findings: Online Survey, Community Transcripts and Focus Group Forum

An online Community of Practice is more than a community of learners

but is a community that learns.

(Schlager, Fusco & Schank, 2002)

Overview

The previous chapters have presented findings from the electronic survey (Chapter 4) and the community discussion transcripts (Chapter 5). This chapter will concern itself with presenting Phase 3 findings and synthesising them with Phase 1 (survey) and Phase 2 (transcripts). It will also discuss the findings from the study in relation to current research and the aims. Phase 3 was a focus-group online forum selected as an instrument that would permit the study to investigate in more detail a number of issues that arose during Phase 1 and 2, this will be explained further and this data will be used to support the discussion findings. The forum questions have provided the scaffolding on which discussion and analysis will be presented in the chapter. It is worthwhile at this point to re-visit the aims of the study. The specific aims of this study are:

1. To investigate online communities of practice as a source of continuous professional development for teachers.
2. To explore the self-sustaining and generative characteristics of online communities.
3. To examine the building of relationships through professional communication.
4. The impact of membership on teacher practice.

This study has concerned itself with the possible role online communities of practice may play in the professional development of teachers. It is therefore important for this chapter to be prefaced with a short summary of the salient features of online communities of practice. The Community of Practice (CoP) was first proposed by Lave and Wenger (1991) and arose from the situated learning field (see Chapter 2). It is an organisational phenomenon (Bond, 2004) which is built around generating knowledge. Lave and Wenger (1991) viewed learning as the process of becoming a member of a CoP and learners move through stages from being a newcomer to becoming an experienced member.

A CoP differs from more traditional conceptualisations of community due, as explained previously in Chapter 2, to the motivation for joining as members display the desire to learn or to extend their knowledge. Community activity is motivated by a need to create new knowledge in order to solve a problem or to expand understanding and when applied to teachers, this motivation may be a solution to a pedagogical dilemma or to acquire new content. An online CoP creates a new sense of place in the user, feelings of disconnectedness, isolation and aloneness are reduced and members do not feel that being in one place cuts them off from other places (Goldberger, 2003). Learning in online CoP occurs primarily through informal interactions among members (Schlager, Fusco, & Schank, 2002) and is a social activity that occurs as new members move through the stages of development interacting with experienced members.

The Internet has provided teachers with opportunities to collaborate and reflect with their peers outside their schools (Hunter, 2002) and facilitates individuals interacting, learning and accessing knowledge and resources within a social space. Online communities of practice are not constrained by time thereby allowing members to move through periods of high to low activity over longer periods (see Table 2.1). The dynamic nature of online membership maintains a freshness and variety that traditional CoPs may not be able to achieve. These features of online communities were apparent and clearly demonstrated by the three communities involved in this study.

Background to focus group forum

The focus-group forum (Phase 3) was developed as an instrument that would permit the study to investigate in more detail a number of issues and questions that arose during the data collection phases 1 and 2 and to provide further clarification in the discussion of the findings. A list of active members from the three online communities was compiled via an analysis of the number of contributions made per member via the community archives over a three month period. The members with the most contributions were invited to participate in the forum and a total of 26 email invitations were sent and 11 responded represents a response rate of 42.31%.

The forum was available for a period of three weeks and this enabled members to re-visit and respond to contributions made by other members. The forum was structured with eight separate discussions with each set up on a separate page. These discussion areas can be seen in Table 6.1. Respondents could scroll down the list of discussion subject areas and choose the ones which interested them. It was encouraging to see that most of the respondents participated in all eight forums. A summary of the number of messages per discussion can be seen in Table 6.1:

Table 6.1

Total number of contributions per discussion

Discussion subject area	Number of contributions to discussion
Impact on classroom	10
Relationships	15
Membership	10

Pedagogy	11
Problem solving	17
Continuous professional development	10
Professional communication	14
Professional development	14

Table 6.1 indicates which subjects were more engaging to the forum respondents. Clearly three of the discussion topics, *Impact on classroom* (*n*=10), *Membership* (*n*=10) and *Continuous professional development* (*n*=10) managed to generate one contribution from each respondent and no further discussion or engagement either with the topic nor with contributions from other respondents was made. However, *Problem solving* (*n*=17) resulted in several respondents re-visiting the discussion thread and commenting on or responding to other contributions. Three topics generated a similar response, but on a smaller scale. These were *Relationships* (*n*=15), *Professional communication* (*n*=14) and *Professional development* (*n*=14). These three topics emerged voluntarily from the data as having particular importance to the respondents and it can be seen below that research has also emphasised these elements.

The eight discussion topics were taken from issues that arose during the survey and transcript analysis. These were either areas or issues that needed further clarification or issues that were not discussed in enough depth to form any conclusions. These eight topics and the questions used to start the discussion will be discussed in more detail within the context of the discussion in this chapter. The messages from the focus-group forum that are cited in this chapter have been coded for easier manipulation. For example, a message taken from the Impact on classroom discussion would have the code, IOC: 2. The number at the end of the code indicates the order the message was contributed to the discussion, so for this example, it was the second message posted to the forum. The codes for each discussion area can be seen in Table 6.2.

Table 6.2

Abbreviated codes for focus-group forum subject areas.

Discussion subject area	Code
Impact on classroom	IOC
Relationships	R
Membership	M
Pedagogy	P
Problem solving	PS
Continuous professional development	CPD
Professional communication	PC
Professional development	PD

The discussion presented in this chapter will be structured according to the eight topics from the focus-group forum (Phase 3):

1. Impact on classroom
2. Relationships
3. Membership
4. Pedagogy
5. Problem solving
6. Continuous professional development
7. Professional communication
8. Professional Development

1. Impact on classroom

Review of research

The majority of current PD programs appear to be failing to achieve any impact on the classroom or changes to teaching practices (Guskey, 2002, p. 58). Teachers are seeking practical skills that will result in positive change in student learning (Guskey, 2002, p. 59) and this is not being provided by current programs. Online communities offer teachers a forum to discuss change and gather evidence, mainly anecdotal, of how successful a change was in a classroom (Galland, 2002). This offers teachers feedback on the potential of new practical skills and helps them to affect change more readily.

It has been suggested that there is a perceived unwillingness amongst teachers to use research or implement suggestions by outside experts (Guskey, 1985, 1986, 2002; Richardson, 1992; Richardson & Placier, 2001) thus PD programs of this nature are less likely to have an impact on the classroom. The resistance to outside experts is removed in online communities as change is initiated and supported by peers and participation.

Evidence found in survey and community transcript analysis

Teachers' desire to seek new practices that result in positive changes to student learning was evidenced by the statements they ranked highly regarding the aims of PD programs. The survey respondents were asked to rank eight statements about PD aims. They ranked "Positive change to teaching practice" first which achieved 34.69% of the responses followed closely by the second-ranked statement "An improvement in student learning" which achieved 33.67% of all responses (n=98). These two ranked aims would support the suggestion that teachers are looking for evidence of positive change to student learning (Guskey, 2002) before new skills or knowledge learnt are adopted and result in change to teaching practice (Guskey, 2002; Richardson, 1990).

The emphasis on improving student learning was also evident when the respondents were asked to provide reasons for maintaining their membership to their online community. The answers that were broadly grouped under two headings; professional requirements and emotional support. The professional requirements category was further divided into classroom/student needs and PD needs. Respondents whose answers fit in the classroom/students needs grouping commonly cited reasons such as access to subject-specific resources, handy hints for the classroom, new relevant content, access to expertise to solve classroom problems, sharing lesson ideas and support for classroom problems. These answers demonstrate that teachers are placing a high priority on acquiring practical skills that may result in improved learning in their classroom. These findings are further supported by the results from the community transcript analysis, where 225 coded messages were found that supported these conclusions (see Figure 6.1). These were messages that were seeking or presenting information about specific pedagogical concerns.

The perceived unwillingness amongst teachers to use research or implement suggestions by outside experts (Guskey, 1985, 1986, 2002; Richardson, 1992; Richardson & Placier, 2001) and the desire to learn from peers and in a participatory manner was demonstrated by the respondents to the survey who indicated a clear preference for face-to-face courses (53.05%) of all responses (Table 4.6). The desire for participatory learning with peers was also clearly shown by the selection of responses that included the term "colleagues" collecting 65.29% of all responses irrespective of whether this was face-to-face or electronic. These community transcripts findings also supported these conclusions with 418 coded messages found that sustain these conclusions (see Figure 6.1). These messages were indicative of a peer group participating in a learning activity, for example offering a suggestion to a problem.

Key research findings for Impact on classroom	Coded messages from community transcript analysis that support research findings	No. of messages per code
		(N=546)
Seeking practical skills the result in improved student learning (Guskey, 2002)	E1 Recognising the problem	37
	I4 Suggestions for consideration	32
	T4 Creating solutions	102
	C1 Vicarious application to the real world	30
	C2 Testing solutions	12
	C3 Defending solutions	12
Unwillingness to use advice from outside experts, a preference	E1 Recognising the problem	37

for learning from peers and a more participatory approach (Guskey, 1985; 1986; 2002; Richardson, 1992; Richardson & Placier, 2001)	E2 Sense of puzzlement	64
	I4 Suggestions for consideration	32
	I5 Brainstorming	15
	T1 Convergence – among group members	74
	T2 Convergence – within a single message	32
	T3 Connecting ideas, synthesis	62
	T4 Creating solutions	102

Figure 6.1: *Coded messages from community transcript analysis that support impact on classroom.*

Evidence found in focus group forum

The focus group forum was asked if they had used any ideas from community discussions or activities in their classroom in an effort to discover if their membership had any impact on their classrooms. This question generated 10 contributions from the respondents (*n*=11) and there were some comments that built on or agreed to earlier postings. The contributions to this question were a combination of personal opinion, regarding what the impact of the online community was on their classroom activities and examples of how they have incorporated community ideas into their pedagogical practice. The comments made by the respondents appear to support the conclusion that teachers were seeking practical skills and evidence of positive change in student learning as proposed by the research. For example:

- "The whole point of the discussions you get here, compared with professional journals, is that it is practical and to the point" (IOC: 2)
- "When I have a problem I need answers quickly and the discussion groups are as quick as it gets. With such a diverse group you get a wider range of alternatives/solutions from around the globe" (IOC:3)
- "Some of my best ideas for the classroom have been spawned from ideas that I never would have come across in the 'real world'" (IOC:7)
- "Ideas, teaching strategies, websites, technical issues for my classroom have been a great part of being in a discussion list – think the collective wisdom of groups helps you develop as a teacher"(IOC: 11)

The second issue proposed by the literature (see Figure 6.1) was that teachers were resistant to outside experts and preferred a more participatory peer-led learning experience. From the comments made by respondents, this would appear to be confirmed:

- "There's nearly always someone with the answer you need" (IOC: 3)
- "Sharing and discussion of new ideas is arguably the greatest benefit of professional community discussions" (IOC: 5)

- "The collective wisdom of groups helps you develop as a teacher" (IOC: 11)

Clearly the respondents have confirmed that they had used ideas from the community discussion in their classroom and that they respond positively to a participatory peer-led learning experience. Thus it could be suggested that there is a positive effect on classroom activities associated with membership to an online community.

This section has clearly shown that teachers have been able to successfully find new practices that result in positive changes to student learning via membership to online communities. This was evident from the results collected via the survey, transcript analysis and forum transcripts. It was also clear that teachers were seeking participatory learning activities with their peers and not programs conducted by outside experts. Teachers are placing great emphasis on practical knowledge that is well-grounded in authentic environments which they can access through experienced, professional peers.

2. Relationships

Review of research

Membership to an online community can help facilitate the building and maintaining of professional relationships and it enables people to communicate with those they would not normally have access to (Hawkes, 1999). Technology has enabled knowledge dissemination and access to learning resources in a global sense (Sorensen & Takle, 2004) and this has had an impact on the professional relationships that are able to be formed. ICTs enable communication by building a community of learners among teachers (Sorensen & Takle, 2004; Teasley & Roschelle, 1993; Watts & Castle, 1992) and these professional relationships that have been formed, can have an impact on pedagogical practice and on professional development. They are no longer limited to a particular school or staffroom but cross traditional 'teaching barriers' such as subject area, grade, school level, speciality, years of service and geographical restrictions. Professional relationships are now global and this has a potential impact on teachers.

Evidence found in survey and community transcript analysis

Membership to an online community aids in the building and maintaining of relationships with people not normally accessible. This simple fact is demonstrated by all of the messages sent and received by an online community (Table 6.3) as they all indicate a relationship present between members by their simple being. As shown in the results from the survey the spread of ages (see Table 4.2) ranged from 20-29 years to over 60 years, and the teaching backgrounds were diverse (see Table 4.3). Members of online communities are exposed to more diversity than is normally found in their personal workplace. The membership cohort of each of the online communities contained a mix of teaching backgrounds, experience, age, locations (urban and rural) and perhaps even nationalities.

When the respondents were asked to explain why they maintained their membership, the fact that it enabled networking was identified by many. This networking capability suggests that not only are teachers able to communicate with peers not normally accessible but that those lines of communication remain constant and allow professional networks to develop. This professional network is also illustrative of a community of learners. These lines of communication are clearly evident by the messages analysed in the community transcript analysis. The number of messages per descriptor can be seen in Table 6.3 below.

A further reason the respondents to the survey identified for maintaining their membership was the emotional support that online communities provide teachers. These included such affective outcomes as enjoying input from other teachers, passing on information, the ability to ask for help, the collegial support, the warm environment, the professional stimulation, "the safety-net – there if needed," a sense of belonging and camaraderie.

Table 6.3

Coded messages from community transcript analysis that support research findings.

Key research findings for Relationships	Coded messages from community transcript analysis that support research findings	No. of messages per code
		(N=546)
Membership to an online community aids in the building and maintaining of relationships (Hawkes, 1999)	E1 Recognising the problem	37
	E2 Sense of puzzlement	64
	I1 Divergence – within the online community	26
Communication is global and offers a wider scope (Sorensen & Takle, 2004)	I2 Divergence – within a single message	9
	I3 Information exchange	17
ICTs enable the building of a community of learners among teachers (Sorensen & Takle,	I4 Suggestions for consideration	32
	I5 Brainstorming	15

2004; Teasley & Roschelle, 1993; Watts & Castle, 1992)	I6	Leaps to conclusions	22
	T1	Convergence – among group members	74
	T2	Convergence – within a single message	32
	T3	Connecting ideas, synthesis	62
	T4	Creating solutions	102
	C1	Vicarious application to the real world	30
	C2	Testing solutions	12
	C3	Defending solutions	12

Evidence found in focus group forum

The focus group forum was asked if they had formed any closer personal relationships with other members in an effort to understand the impact their membership had on forming professional relationships. This question generated 15 contributions from the respondents, who again largely responded to the question rather than to other respondents' contributions. Overwhelmingly all respondents stated that they had formed relationships online that had spilled over into communication outside of the community. This shift to 'real world' contact did not appear to undermine the value placed on online relationships.

- "The professional relationships that can be developed online are just as rewarding, whether you ever meet or not" (R:8)
- "The physical meeting is not all that important; the virtual community is really enough. While it's really nice to meet someone face to face, see the family, enjoy time together, it's not essential" (R:11)

It has been shown that membership to an online community aids in the building and maintaining of relationships. It facilitates networking that provides the opportunity for teachers to have access to a wider peer group that stretches across curriculum, subject areas and location. It also provides teachers with emotional support that helps them to face issues or problems in their professional lives.

3. Membership

Review of research

It was suggested in Chapter 2 that the most commonly found forms of online communities may display characteristics of a new hybrid grouping of community. Kaufman (1959) proposed two

137

polar ideologies one that was homogeneous, and had face-to-face contact and the second was cosmopolitan, anonymous and had mass contacts. The new hybrid form of community was characterised as homogenous in purpose, dynamic mass membership and participatory and lacking traditional face-to-face contact. A review of the literature defining community revealed that an online community is reliant upon the interaction between the collective, operational, personal and manifest components (see Figure 2.1).

Membership to an online CoP, if it is examined purely from the perspective proposed by Lave and Wenger (1991) is characterised by members moving through stages from being a newcomer to becoming an experienced member. As members move through these stages they increasingly become involved in the learning and knowledge-building activities of the community.

Evidence found in survey and community transcript analysis

As previously noted an online community is reliant upon the interaction between the collective, operational, personal and manifest components (Figure 2.1). In an effort to clarify if the three online communities involved in this study displayed these components, an informal survey of their features were conducted and the results can be seen in Figure 6.1. It is apparent that all three posses all four components and can thus be considered as positive examples of online communities.

Collective components	**Manifest components**
Common goals and group purposes	*Collaborative, collective and self-regulatory*
✓ BECTA – **Top Teachers** (Clearly stated in description and membership application)	✓ BECTA – **Top Teachers** (self-evident via transcript analysis)
✓ SSABSA – **English Teachers** (Briefly described in general description of group)	✓ SSABSA – **English Teachers** (self-evident via transcript analysis)
✓ OzTeacherNet (Clearly stated on front page of community website)	✓ OzTeacherNet(self-evident via transcript analysis)
Operational components	**Personal components**
Common space, collective rules and behaviours	*Individuals developing into members of a community*
✓ BECTA – **Top Teachers** (clear common space, rules and behaviours are implicit and informal)	✓ BECTA – **Top Teachers** (evident from results from survey, transcripts and forum)
✓ SSABSA – **English Teachers** (clear common space, rules and behaviours are implicit and informal)	✓ SSABSA – **English Teachers** (evident from results from survey, transcripts and forum)
✓ OzTeacherNet(clear common space, rules and behaviours are implicit and informal)	✓ OzTeacherNet (evident from results from survey, transcripts and forum)

Figure 6.1: Audit of the components that define an online community using the three online communities involved in the study.

The online communities involved in the study all clearly demonstrated a homogenous purpose, they were concerned with a particular aspect of teaching, for example English teaching (SSABSA), the use of ICT in teaching (BECTA) and professional communication between teachers (OTN). These conclusions can be evidenced by the content of the triggering messages (Evocative coded messages) from the transcript analysis. These messages ($n=101$) were homogenous and appropriate for the online community they were posted to (see Table 6.4).

The survey discovered that membership and participation, within these aspects was largely directed by the topic the community was discussing. Member activity fluctuates and this is generally dependent on outside pressure. This was evidenced by the statement the majority of respondents selected that best described their membership, "My participation depends on the topic being discussed by the list, I participate more if I am interested in the topic" 54.08% (see Table 4.16). It also indicated that members were seeking personally relevant topics to motivate them to participate and that they did not feel the need to comment on all topics raised or respond to questions asked but only participate when they have a particular interest or expertise to share.

The desire for a participatory mode of learning (and indicative of the characteristics of situated learning) was demonstrated by one of the reasons the respondents identified as evidence of membership to online communities representing PD. They suggested that it encouraged active learning. The transcript analysis provided ample evidence that a participatory approach to learning was present in the online communities. This was evident by the number of inquisitive and tentative messages that were made in response to an evocative message (see Table 6.4). This participation amongst members is more clearly presented in the thread pattern analysis where graphical representations of this participatory activity is presented. The participatory approach of a community may switch between flowchart, regular cluster or bonded cluster depending on the complexity of the discussion thread and needs of the community (see Chapter 5).

The stages of membership that have been proposed by Lave and Wenger (1991) were not evident in the results from the survey. However, they were apparent in the results from the transcript analysis and focus-group forum. As can be seen in Table 6.4, there were a number of messages ($n=35$) that demonstrated this movement through different membership stages. These were divergent messages that portrayed members who were learning the processes of community activities (I1) and those who were reaching an understanding of the learning activity being undertaken (I2).

Table 6.4

Coded messages from community transcript analysis that support research findings.

Key research findings for Membership	Coded messages from community transcript analysis that support research findings	No. of messages per code
		(N=546)
Online communities are homogenous, have dynamic mass membership and are participatory (adapted from Kaufman, 1959)	E1 Recognising the problem	37
	E2 Sense of puzzlement	64
Members move through stages of membership, from newcomer to experienced member (Lave & Wenger, 1991)	I1 Divergence – within the online community	26
	I2 Divergence – within a single message	9
	I3 Information exchange	17
	I4 Suggestions for consideration	32
	I5 Brainstorming	15
	I6 Leaps to conclusions	22
	T1 Convergence – among group members	74
	T2 Convergence – within a single message	32
	T3 Connecting ideas, synthesis	62
	T4 Creating solutions	102

Evidence found in focus group forum

The focus group forum was asked how they would describe their initial presence in the community and if this presence had changed. This question was designed to determine if the respondents moved through the stages from being a newcomer to becoming an experienced member as proposed by Lave and Wenger (1991) and if they felt their level of membership influenced their level of learning and participation. This question generated 11 contributions from the respondents and the answers to the question were personal responses, not responses to other postings. Some postings did refer to sharing similar feelings to other respondents, but generally it was an explanation of their personal journey to becoming full and active members of the list. Many reflected on how they first felt like an outsider, as the following examples demonstrate:

- "I was so nervous when I entered my first query – but my nervousness left the instant I saw replies" (M: 2)
- "I guess I lurked for a short while...working out how people asked questions (M:2)
- "You feel as awkward as you do when you walk into a new school or workplace for the first time" (M:3)
- "Initially I lurk on a list to get a feel for the other participants but eventually you acquire the 'courage' or is it the 'urge' to make a reply or request" (M:11)

This initial lurking behaviour is interesting to see described, as the respondents to this forum were invited to participate because they were active, vigorous members of their online communities. It would seem to support the idea that members go through stages, initially as a newcomer, to a full participating member (Lave & Wenger, 1991). This process of slowly engaging in the learning activities of the community is best summarised by the following posting:

- "At first I felt that I am at the edge, just looking in. It takes some time to get a sense of how things operate and to establish myself as a member. Most often that happens when I am able to contribute something of value to the conversation. From there I become more comfortable and begin to feel part of the group – a contributing member" (M:6)

It is apparent that members of online communities move through the stages of membership that have been suggested by Lave and Wenger (1991). They appear change their membership status from lurker or browser, to active participant depending on the topic under discussion and their learning needs. This fluctuating activity is also dependent on outside pressures and the relevancy of topics. It is apparent via the evidence collected from the survey and transcripts that the members are engaging in a participatory and active mode of learning, and this was further supported by the forum transcripts.

4. Pedagogy

Review of research

As mentioned previously, teaching (pedagogy) is in a constant of change (Richardson, 1992) and pedagogical practices are continually absorbing new skills and knowledge. As a result, it has been suggested that teachers are self-regulatory (Gallimore et al., 1986) and that pedagogical practice may be in a process of constant adjustment as teachers respond to triggers to acquire skills or learn new instructional strategies (Gallimore et al., 1986).

If pedagogy is responding to the self-regulatory practices of teachers, then online communities may help to build teacher professionalism as teachers start to recognize their own expertise (Hawkes, 1999). Technology has made possible a geographically accessible electronic manifestation of Lave and Wenger's (1991) conceptualisation of communities of practice and as such through strategies such as collaboration, cooperation, discourse and interaction with peers (Hawkes,

1999; Merseth & Lacey, 1993; Watts & Castle, 1992) it has the potential of having a huge impact on pedagogy.

Evidence found in survey and community transcript analysis

As evidence of the constant state of change and the need to learn new skills faced by the teaching profession, the majority of the respondents to the survey reported that they were required to fulfil or at least demonstrate that they had achieved a certain number of PD hours per year. There was a broad range of answers which defied comparative analysis and could range from 2 days to 40 hours per year. Generally respondents viewed this requirement positively but some complained that the mandated requirements made PD tedious, irrelevant, insufficient and "open to rorting." Many respondents reported that they sought further courses outside of (additional to) the quota or the required PD program and set themselves PD quotas based on specific areas or skills. This may indicate that current PD systems are failing to meet their needs or that they are displaying a high level of professionality. The constant state of change faced by teachers is demonstrated by the number of messages (*n=165*) that support this finding in Table 6.5 below. These were evocative and inquisitive messages and supported the idea that members were exploring some aspect of change, for example, puzzling over a classroom issue.

When asked what the aims of PD should be, respondents positioned "Obtaining new skills or knowledge" in third position which confirms suggestions by research that teaching is constantly changing and new ideas are being continually disseminated throughout the profession. This conclusion is again apparent in Table 6.5 as the evocative and inquisitive messages were mainly concerned with acquiring knowledge or solving problems.

Teacher professionalism was clearly evident in the survey results as it would appear that the respondents learned about their online community via professional means. This expectation is grounded here through the discovery that 32.65% found the community via the expertise of a friend or colleague and 40.82% found it via a link from a professional website. Thus the majority (73.47%) joined the community via professional "introductions" which is indicative of a high sense of professional responsibility and suggestive of a group who recognise their own growing expertise (see Table 4.13). Teacher professionalism and the sense that the online community represented an expert group is also demonstrated by the messages coded in the transcript analysis. Messages that could clearly show this trait (*n= 391*) were coded inquisitive or tentative and were illustrative of a group exploring a problem and reaching a solution. These messages can be seen in Table 6.5.

This emerging understanding of their own expertise and that of the online community could also been seen in the reasons cited for maintaining their membership. It was a popularly cited that members saw the online community fulfilling a PD role as this was provided as a reason for maintaining their membership. It was further clarified as the opportunity to learn from other teachers/peers, access to like-minded professionals, engage in professional discussions, share professional knowledge, "keep up with current professional trends," and a desire to be "professional in my role." All of these traits are representative of teacher professionalism and recognition of their own expertise. This pooling of expertise is also demonstrative of the building of collective knowledge by the online community.

Associated with this desire for professionalism was the capacity online community membership had to remove geographical limitations with some respondents suggesting it was one of the only ways teachers in remote locations could maintain their professional learning. As stated previously this emerged as a critical finding in the study and it is clear that teachers are actively looking for opportunities to develop their own teaching practices. Evidence of this can be seen in Table 6.5 via the messages demonstrating collaboration with peers. This communication is not constrained by geographical limitations.

Due to pedagogical practice constantly changing and responding to triggers, change or access to it needs to be easy and fast. When asked if membership to online communities represented meaningful PD, respondents confirmed that an advantage was the immediacy and relevancy. A further advantage was that responses are fast, solutions are created quickly and topics can be discussed rapidly. When a teacher responds to a trigger and seeks a remedy, it could be a simple need for information or a solution to a problem. The messages that demonstrated the presence of self-regulated learning (that is, in response to a trigger) can be seen in Table 6.5 (n=295). A further feature associated with this was the fact that the professional dialogue was with peers outside of their workplace which ensured wider experience.

In an effort to determine if membership did result in changes to pedagogy, the respondents were asked if they had changed any of their teaching practices as a result of participating in the online community. Seventy-seven percent of respondents answered positively to this question with many able to provide examples to support this idea. An aspect that is closely related to this effect of change was the relevancy of the subject matter that it was linked closely to real life, was targeted to their needs and was authentic.

Table 6.5

Coded messages from community transcript analysis that support research findings.

Key research findings for Pedagogy	Coded messages from community transcript analysis that support research findings	No. of messages per code
		(N=546)

Teaching (pedagogy) is in a state of constant change (Richardson, 1992)	E1 Recognising the problem	37
	E2 Sense of puzzlement	64
	I3 Information exchange	17
	I4 Suggestions for consideration	32
	I5 Brainstorming	15
Teachers are self-regulatory and respond to triggers to acquire new skills (Gallimore et al., 1986)	E1 Recognising the problem	37
	E2 Sense of puzzlement	64
	T3 Connecting ideas, synthesis	62
	T4 Creating solutions	102
	C1 Vicarious application to the real world	30
Online communities help to build teacher professionalism as teachers start to recognize their own expertise (Hawkes, 1999)	I1 Divergence – within the online community	26
	I2 Divergence – within a single message	9
	I3 Information exchange	17
	I4 Suggestions for consideration	32
	I5 Brainstorming	15
	I6 Leaps to conclusions	22
	T1 Convergence – among group members	74
	T2 Convergence – within a single message	32
	T3 Connecting ideas, synthesis	62
	T4 Creating solutions	102
Collaboration and interaction with peers (Hawkes, 1999; Merseth & Lacey, 1993; Watts & Castle, 1992) has a huge impact on pedagogy	I3 Information exchange	17
	T1 Convergence – among group members	74
	T2 Convergence – within a single message	32

T3	Connecting ideas, synthesis	62
T4	Creating solutions	102
C1	Vicarious application to the real world	30
C2	Testing solutions	12
C3	Defending solutions	12

Evidence found in focus group forum

The focus group forum was asked if they had changed any of their teaching practices as a result from what they had learnt in the community. This question was designed to reveal if their pedagogical practices were in fact constantly adjusting to new skills and knowledge and if there was a sense of teacher professionalism or learning from peer-experts. This question generated 11 contributions from the respondents and there was a sense of building on what the other respondents had stated in their contributions rather than being a series of independent answers to the questions. There was a consensus that pedagogical practise had changed as a result of membership to online communities. The following examples are indicative of the respondents' contributions:

- "Yes again – and not only in the areas where I've asked for help. Just following threads makes you stop and think about things you hadn't thought of before – and some of these have seen me do a complete turnaround in what I thought was 'right' " (P:2)
- "Without a doubt my classroom practice is informed by participation in online communities" (P:5)
- "Can you imagine being a teacher and not understanding things like pedagogy or constructivism? That was me. What else didn't I understand? What else do I still not understand? Man, I *need* to belong to online communities or I'd just be a really ignorant jackass of a teacher" (P:7)
- "Boy, have I EVER learned a lot and has it changed my teaching. I can't imagine standing in front of a class of students being the font of all knowledge. I started teaching 45 years ago, when that is what you were taught to do!" (P:8)

As it has been noted, teaching is in a constant state of change and teachers are faced with a continuous need to learn new skills and current PD programs are failing to meet this need. This need was identified as a priority for teachers who responded to the survey and it was also apparent that teachers are self-regulatory. Teacher professionalism was evident from the results of the survey and transcript analysis and there was a clear recognition of the expertise of the community, as a source of professional learning. The interaction between members was shown to directly affect pedagogy, as resultant examples of changes to practices were provided.

5. Problem Solving

Review of research

Problem solving is an example of constructing knowledge and engaging in learning. When a member poses a problem to their online community, it is because they wish for help to find a solution. Clearly, the members of that community represent a social collective and the activities they embark on together to create a solution or new knowledge is an illustration of a social collective constructing meaning together. The theory of situated learning views activity as central to learning and cognition (Brown, Collins, & Duguid, 1989; Greeno, 1998; Putnam & Borko, 2000) and this activity must be embedded in authentic situations otherwise the knowledge created is false (Brown et al., 1989). Generally, the activity observed in online communities frequented by teachers appears to be inspired from professional inquiries, classroom problems or the quest for new skills.

Evidence found in survey and community transcript analysis

The online community represents a problem solving resource for members and there were 227 messages found in the transcript analysis that supported this finding (see Table 6.6). It was clear from the types of coded messages that illustrate this resource that members were looking for solutions to problems and applications to the real world. It is important to note the influence that the years of teaching experience the group has on this aspect. As shown in the survey the respondents represented a group of highly experienced teachers with the majority having over 20 years experience (n=59, representing 60.2% of all survey respondents), hence the social collective possess considerable authority. These activities were keenly demonstrated by the messages that were coded during the transcript analysis (n=222), as seen in Table 6.6. The group activities were not simple problem-solution discussions, but were the detailed negotiations of a learning activity, as demonstrated by divergent messages (I1 and I2) and information exchange messages (I3).

Table 6.6

Coded messages from community transcript analysis that support research findings.

Key research findings for Problem solving	Coded messages from community transcript analysis that support research findings	No. of messages per code
		(N=546)
Problem solving is an example of constructing knowledge and engaging in learning.	E1 Recognising the problem	37
	I4 Suggestions for consideration	32
	T4 Creating solutions	104
	C1 Vicarious application to the real world	30

	C2 Testing solutions	12
	C3 Defending solutions	12
An online community is a social collective constructing meaning together and activity as central to learning (Brown, Collins, & Duguid, 1989; Greeno, 1998; Putnam & Borko, 2000)	E1 Recognising the problem	37
	E2 Sense of puzzlement	64
	I1 Divergence – within the online community	26
	I2 Divergence – within a single message	9
	I3 Information exchange	17
	I4 Suggestions for consideration	32
	I5 Brainstorming	15
	I6 Leaps to conclusions	22
	T1 Convergence – among group members	74
	T2 Convergence – within a single message	32
	T3 Connecting ideas, synthesis	62
	T4 Creating solutions	102
	C1 Vicarious application to the real world	30
	C2 Testing solutions	12
	C3 Defending solutions	12

Evidence found in focus group forum

The focus group forum were asked if they used the online community as a problem solving resource in an attempt to understand the types of activities online communities engaged in and if it could be equated with the situated view of learning. It was hoped that this question would provide clear evidence of a social collective constructing meaning together. This question generated 17 messages from the respondents and was the most contributed discussion topic. All the contributions agreed that they used the online community as a problem solving resource. Many contributions gave specific examples of how that has been achieved, some have explained further why they see it as a useful tool for this purpose.

- "Without doubt – online communities for me are valuable resources that put me in touch with people who know more about stuff than I do – I happily say I do not know how to do something and throw myself on the mercy of the list, sadly, too, many others will not risk that for fear of appearing less than they would like – nothing ventured, nothing gained is my online motto" (PS:7)

- "As a problem solving source they are fantastic – there is always someone who knows something...that regularly doesn't happen at school!" (PS:3)
- "I think a professional....a true professional continues to learn/share/collaborate" (PS:6)
- "A group has the combined knowledge to greatly increase the ability to solve problems compared to an individual. Different members of the group will approach a problem in different ways and will bring different points of view and skills to the problem" (PS:16)

The concept of the online community being used as a resource was described as a give-and-take process. As one respondent concluded:

- "Being part of a community is a two-way street. If I think I can help with a question that somebody asks then I'll usually offer some comments – unless somebody else has already said all that I could say. On the other hand, being an occasional contributor makes me feel better about asking for advice or assistance when I need it. I don't do either very often but it's certainly a resource that I'm aware of and sometimes suggest to others looking for answers" (PS: 8)

The online community represents a problem solving resource for members that was used to find solutions to pedagogical dilemmas and practical applications to authentic environments. It was clear from the evidence collected via the survey, transcripts and forum that members used this function frequently and perceived as a positive source of professional support.

6. Continuous Professional Development

Review of research

It has been previously suggested that the teaching profession is in a constant state of change as new ideas or developments are disseminated (Borko, Mayfield, Marion, Flexer, & Cumbro, 1997; Gallimore, Dalton, & Tharp, 1986; Richardson, 1990, 1992, 1994, 1997; Richardson & Placier, 2001) and all of these new ideas and developments need to be absorbed into the classroom. There is a perceived requirement for an ongoing, continuous form of professional development (Richardson, 1992). To ensure participants successfully engage in the learning process, the content must address the needs of the teachers, not as more commonly observed, the needs as discerned by school management or higher (Sorge & Russell, 2000). It has also been suggested that the focus of PD programs should be on providing teachers with a basis for continual growth and problem-solving (Franke et al., 1998) and this would become a basis for self-sustaining and generative change (Franke et al., 1998), thus meeting the constant need for new skills faced by teachers.

Evidence found in survey and community transcript analysis

As stated previously, new ideas constantly need to be absorbed by teachers, this is not a supposition by research but a fact supported by the findings of the transcript analysis. The number of messages that indicated the presence of change, either in the form of a problem, suggestion or issue for consideration clearly supported this phenomenon (n=180) as seen in Table 6.7. The literature has concluded that there is a need for an ongoing and continuous form of PD. However, the results of the survey would indicate that whilst longer programs, 2-3 months are the most favoured (40.82%), long-term programs, 6 months or longer scored only 20.41% (see Table 4.8). This would suggest that teachers themselves have not yet recognised this need or their opinions have been influenced by previous poor PD experiences. However, four respondents commented that the most effective model for change was "continuous and ongoing" PD and that this "is the real benefit of [learning] online." Continuous and ongoing PD, can be facilitated easily by online methods, but it would appear to contradict the desired "face-to-face, colleagues not from workplace and conducted away from workplace" criteria determined by the responses to questions in the survey.

An indication of continuous and ongoing PD is the length of membership respondents had to their community. The predominant responses were 1–3 years and 4-6 years (each returning 34.69% of all responses). The outlying results were those who belonged to the online community for longer than 6 years (14.28%) and those who had been a member for less than 1 year (15.31%). The average length of membership is 3 years, which would indicate that PD can be sustained over a longer period of time and can be ongoing and continuous. As noted in the discussion on the number of subscriptions held, membership to a community requires a commitment of time and energy hence if members did not feel such a membership was worthwhile, that is, able to satisfy their needs, it would be expected that they would "drop off" fairly quickly. From the results of the transcript analysis, there would appear to be evidence to support the suggestion that online communities are self-sustaining and generative. The presence of messages that can be coded as all four descriptors or phases of learning would indicate that the learning is generative. All of the messages coded (n=546) in the transcript analysis collectively demonstrates this hence we could suppose that Table 6.7 presents evidence of sustainability being present in online communities.

Perhaps one feature that would directly influence the ability for online communities to be a continuous source of PD for teachers are ICT abilities. The self-rated confidence in using ICTs that was reported in the survey ranged from competent to professionally competent (98.08%) with only one respondent (1.02%) indicating a poor level of confidence in using ICT. Seventy-one respondents (72.45%) indicated a confidence level which was either highly or professionally competent. This may be influential factor in the impact that membership to online communities can play in accessing continuous PD.

149

Table 6.7

Coded messages from community transcript analysis that support research findings.

Key research findings for Continuous PD	Coded messages from community transcript analysis that support research findings	No. of messages per code
		(N=546)
New ideas are constantly being disseminated and need to be absorbed (Borko, Mayfield, Marion, Flexer, & Cumbro, 1997; Gallimore, Dalton, & Tharp, 1986)	E1 Recognising the problem	37
	E2 Sense of puzzlement	64
	I3 Information exchange	17
	T3 Connecting ideas, synthesis	62
PD should provide a basis for self-sustaining and generative change (Franke et al., 1998) to meet the constant need for new skills faced by teachers.	E1 Recognising the problem	37
	E2 Sense of puzzlement	64
	I1 Divergence – within the online community	26
	I2 Divergence – within a single message	9
	I3 Information exchange	17
	I4 Suggestions for consideration	32
	I5 Brainstorming	15
	I6 Leaps to conclusions	22
	T1 Convergence – among group members	74
	T2 Convergence – within a single message	32
	T3 Connecting ideas, synthesis	62
	T4 Creating solutions	102
	C1 Vicarious application to the real world	30
	C2 Testing solutions	12
	C3 Defending solutions	12

Evidence found in focus group forum

In an effort to determine if the on-going continuous nature of online communities was perceived as an advantage, the focus group were invited to comment on this aspect. It was hoped that the respondents might make a connection between this characteristic and their continuous need to learn new skills. This question generated 10 contributions from the respondents and was one of the least popular discussion topics. The brevity of this discussion, which was limited to a contribution from each of the respondents participating in the forum, may be explained by the consensus the group reached on this topic. All of the contributions agreed that the on-going continuous nature of online communities was an advantage. Their explanations might be summarised by the following contribution:

- "The on-going continuous nature of online communities is a big advantage as you know that at any time or place you can log on ask a question, make a statement post a resource and someone else will reply with a positive or negative response that will help clarify your thinking. Love the collective wisdom of the group" (CPD:11)

The community's role in their potential need to accommodate change may be best surmised by the following posting:

- "I take what interests me, pick at some of the stuff I am not too sure about, and don't bother too much with the stuff that doesn't really grab me. I can engage with, or ignore the stream of ideas in whatever way I choose. The important thing is that I have a steady stream of ideas coming past me every day" (CPD: 7)

It was evident that membership to an online community represented access and participation in continuous and ongoing PD. Membership had been maintained for an average of three years which equals a significant period of time engaged in professional learning. The online communities also appeared to be self-sustaining and generative and may help to explain why membership is maintained. The community activities are grounded in authenticity and it was shown that they have a great potential to accommodate change.

7. Professional Communication

Review of research

Computer-mediated communication (CMC) has provided learners with a new context for professional communication. A CMC-based community allows participants to communicate in an environment that encourages discussions beyond physical limitations and provides a fresh learning domain which enables new and different forms of educational interactions (White, 2003). They are readily accessible, not hindered by opening hours or other such constraints and offers flexibility not previously available to collaborative learning activities. These new opportunities for professional communication occur largely via the written word and are characteristically more informal and colloquial in nature.

CMC has some unique behaviours such as lurking or browsing associated with it. The levels of participation among members of a community can vary widely (Wild, 1999) and new members tend to lurk around the edges of the community learning how to become a member. These are demonstrative of the stages of learning suggested by Lave and Wenger (1991). It was noted in Chapter 2 that the literature in this field has identified four advantages associated with CMC-based learning (Pachler, 2001; Salmon, 2000; Wood, 2003). These were:

i.   CMC encourages discussion by facilitating more opportunities for individuals to express their ideas
ii.   CMC secures fast transmission which allows instant feedback and the ability to save and revisit data
iii. CMC allows time for reflection and considered response
iv.   Written communication results in the participation of all group members equally, for example, active contributors and lurkers

It has also been suggested that teachers lack the opportunities for professional communication, such as to share their thinking and construct new knowledge about their teaching practices (Merseth & Lacey, 1993; Watts & Castle, 1992) and online communities can help to overcome this. This potential for increased professional communication can result in substantive changes to teaching practices (Hawkes, 1999; Hoadley & Pea, 2002; Marx, Blumenfeld, & Krajcik, 1998; Watts & Castle, 1992). Teachers are exposed to new ideas and can receive peer support and feedback as they attempt to understand new ideas and use them in their own teaching practices (Merseth & Lacey, 1993; Watts & Castle, 1992).

Evidence found in survey and community transcript analysis

Online communities represent a new context for teachers to engage in professional communication. The effectiveness of this and the positive reaction from members to this feature are demonstrated by two factors. The first is the number of online community memberships they hold, as they may indicate a desire for professional communication and the opportunity to change teaching practices. The majority of respondents, 56.12%, were members of 1 to 3 online communities (see Table 4.10), whilst the second largest grouping indicated that 22.45% were members of 4 to 6 online communities. The second factor that demonstrated an engagement in professional communication are the messages themselves. The transcript analysis resulted in 118 messages (Table 6.8) that were indicative of teachers engaging in communication, these were simple trigger messages, but in fact the total number of messages per community (*N*=546) would underlie this point.

It was established, via a Pearson chi-square analysis (see Table 4.11) that an influential relationship existed between the number of years teaching experience and the number of online community memberships an individual held. The highest number of memberships to online communities can be found in the teachers who have over 20 years experience (see Table 4.10), who consistently fall in between the 40-49 and 50-59 age brackets (see Figure 4.1). This demonstrates clearly that teachers are looking for more opportunities for professional communication and that the majority of members are not early career teachers seeking support but are experienced teachers seeking to improve or change their pedagogical practices.

The opportunity to express ideas has been identified as a reason why teachers seek professional communication (Pachler, 2001; Salmon, 2000; Wood, 2003). An online community presents as a forum to share ideas and respond to other members' messages. This is evidenced by the transcript analysis, where 161 coded messages demonstrated this opportunity (Table 6.8). These messages showed expressions of ideas, discussions (not necessarily resulting in a consensus) and connecting ideas together. The opportunity for expression was identified as important by the respondents to the survey who were asked if their membership had met their expectations. This was overwhelmingly answered in the positive with 92.85% agreeing that their expectations had been met and one of the most commonly cited reasons was "there is such freedom in discussion". It was also suggested by a large number of respondents that this opportunity for professional communication had "increased my knowledge of other teaching practices". This desire for opportunities to express ideas was raised in another section of the survey. When asked why they considered their membership to an online community represented meaningful PD it was explained that it encouraged professional conversation. The desire to engage in professional communication and have the opportunity to express ideas were elements that continued to appear in comments collected by the survey.

It has been suggested that CMC allows time for reflection and consideration of responses. When the respondents were asked if they could identify any advantages of participating in online communities as a form of PD, a large number of responses identified time. The ability to log on and participate according to their own schedule was a clear advantage and the asynchronous nature of the communities gave them time to think, reflect and compose answers. The transcript analysis demonstrated this ability via the variety of responses and the evidence of consideration in the messages. There were 252 messages (Table 6.8) that demonstrated this, however unless the time of triggering messages was noted and then compared to the times of the responses from the community it would be difficult to determine how much time and reflection members partake.

Table 6.8

Coded messages from community transcript analysis that support research findings.

Key research findings for Professional communication	Coded messages from community transcript analysis that support research findings	No. of messages per code *(N=546)*
Online communities provide teachers with a new context for professional communication (White, 2003)	E1 Recognising the problem	37
	E2 Sense of puzzlement	64
	I3 Information exchange	17
Teachers are seeking more opportunities to express ideas (Pachler, 2001; Salmon, 2000; Wood, 2003)	I1 Divergence – within the online community	26
	I2 Divergence – within a single message	9
	I3 Information exchange	17
	I4 Suggestions for consideration	32
	I5 Brainstorming	15
	T3 Connecting ideas, synthesis	62
Provides more time for reflection and consideration (Pachler, 2001; Salmon, 2000; Wood, 2003)	I1 Divergence – within the online community	26
	I2 Divergence – within a single message	9
	I3 Information exchange	17
	I4 Suggestions for consideration	32
	T1 Convergence – among group members	74
	T2 Convergence – within a single message	32
	T3 Connecting ideas, synthesis	62

154

Evidence found in focus group forum

The focus group forum were asked to consider the value of professional discussions conducted online in comparison to those conducted in their workplace. It was hoped that they might comment on the differences the online context made to professional communication. This question generated 14 contributions from the respondents. The respondents appeared to cite the ability to engage in professional discussion as one of the key attractions for membership to online communities.

This discussion contained many comments regarding the quality of members in a community affecting the level of professional communication that a list may offer. The following excerpts from messages highlights the ideas that were proposed:

- "I rely on lists to be filled with experienced professionals – I wouldn't bother if they weren't" (PC:3)
- "...because it is online, if you get advice from a flake, you can always say "thanks" and ignore—though that does raise the question: how do you pick the flakes, the nongs and the know-nothings?" (PC:2)

Several posting commented on online community's ability to provide a space for teachers to express their ideas, as illustrated by the following message.

- "It is a place to share successes, express ideas out loud and sharing" (PC:10)

This discussion also highlighted the advantage online communities have in lessening feelings of isolation, regardless of geographical or ideological factors hence providing teachers with more opportunities to express ideas. As the following excerpts show:

- "Being part of a virtual professional community often fills a void in my professional learning as often there may not be someone with like interests available for the discussions needed and the lists can help to fill this gap and stimulate further thinking" (PC:9)
- "The problem is that a workplace – school – will only have a small pool, if any, of colleagues with similar needs. Online communities permit contact with colleagues of similar roles, curriculum areas, experience, etc" (PC:5)
- "In my workplace, I'm an island. There is no one else there like me, so it's only through the virtual community discussions that I can have relevant professional discussions" (PC:12)

The behaviour of lurking and browsing was also commented on by respondents and it was not seen as a negative behaviour. It would appear to be a behaviour that more experienced members of communities employ at times.

- "Often I lurk and sponge off knowledge given by others on the lists. (Yes! I admit it) At other times I am hopefully able to contribute to the learnings of other" (PC:9)
- "As a lurker on many lists, I find professional discussion invaluable even though I tend not to join in." (PC:15)

Online communities are a new context for teachers to engage in professional communication, which in turn provides opportunities to change teaching practices. It was clear via an examination of the results from the survey and transcripts that teachers were seeking more opportunities to express their ideas, and the online communities facilitates this. The asynchronous nature of the medium also allowed members more flexibility with time, allowing for reflection and consideration.

8. Professional Development

Review of research

Professional development for teachers has traditionally been offered as workshops conducted after school by an outside expert or by attending conferences during school holidays. This would appear to be ineffective as research has claimed that short workshops do not encourage the development of new skills nor do they have any long-lasting effect on pedagogy (Boyle, While, & Boyle, 2004; Goldenberg & Gallimore, 1991; Guskey, 2002; Huberman, 2001). What has been suggested is that PD needs to be more complex, long term and embedded in schools (Ingvarson, Meiers, & Beavis, 2003).

It has been suggested that PD programs for teachers should be sustained over a longer period of time and allow more time for teachers to practice what they learn and share their experiences with fellow teachers (Sorge & Russell, 2000). The majority of research has concluded that learning, for teachers, should be conducted collaboratively (Boyle et al., 2004; Goldenberg & Gallimore, 1991; Greeno, 1998; Hargreaves, 1993; Huberman, 2001; Kemmis, 1989; Strehle, Whatley, Kurz, & Hausfather, 2001).

Adult learners display unique characteristics that need to be considered (see Chapter 2). They are independent, internally motivated, self-directed and bring a wealth of experience to the learning environment (Knowles et al., 1998; Lee, 1998). A key feature of adult learning is that it is largely situated and authentic, as it is usually located within the workplace. Learning is an ongoing and inevitable process arising from participation in work practices across working lives (Billet, 2001b) and is not a separately occurring phenomenon.

Online communities offer the advantage of teachers being able to work at their own pace and location (Bronack, Kilbane, Herbert, & McNergney, 1999). Technology has had an effect on the physical location of a professional development program as it shifts away from the workplace affording teachers a flexibility that was not previously available (Barnett, 1999; Billet, 1993, 2001a, 2001b; Hodkinson & Bloomer, 2002; Hodkinson & Hodkinson, 2003; Zahner, 2002).

Evidence found in survey and community transcript analysis

The desire for authentic and relevant PD was clearly indicated by the results from the survey (see Chapter 4) and the transcript analysis (Table 6.9). The courses or workshops that attracted favourable comments were generally subject-specific and thus personally relevant and this demand for authentic and contextualised professional development is consistent with the findings of Lloyd and Cochrane (2006). PD programs that left a favourable impression on respondents can be seen as reflecting the characteristics identified by research as desirable. The respondents were looking for different strategies that could be implemented in the classroom (*authenticity*) and programs that allowed them to participate, present and observe (*collaborative*). The number of messages coded during the transcript analysis that demonstrated authenticity (n=274) and collaborative learning (n=435) can be seen in Table 6.9.

It has been presented that adults present unique characteristics as learners. They demonstrate a higher internal motivation to learn, are self-directed and bring a valuable wealth of experience to the learning event. The appreciation of these unique characteristics are reflected in the survey when the respondents identified teaching staff (87.75%) as the most suitable group for selecting the content of PD. This was also reflected in the content of the messages. It is apparent when the coded messages are examined that many illustrated the 'adult learner' and their specific characteristics (n=425). For example, internal motivation would have been the trigger for evocative messages and the responses to them, self-direction is evidenced by committed messages demonstrating applying knowledge and prior experience would be evidence in the content of all the coded messages (Table 6.9).

With regard to the location and time for PD, the survey indicated that there was a preference for locations away from the workplace, with 70.41% preferring to have PD based away from their workplaces (see Table 4.7). This is easily achieved by online communities and this flexibility has a positive effect on concerns about time. One of the reasons why members believed their membership was a meaningful form of PD was that it was convenient time wise. Members were able to access and participate when it was convenient for them and not at specific prescribed times, more commonly a feature of traditional formalised PD programs. This is clearly evidenced by the total number of messages sent and received by the community due to its accessibility and asynchronous nature (Table 6.9).

The flexibility of time was also evident in the number of hours members spent participating in community activities. The survey found that the majority of members spent between 0-6 hours per week (85.71%) and this can be broken down to (a) less than an hour per week (22.45%), (b) 1-3 hours (37.76%), and (c) 4-6 hours (25.51%). This breaks down to 1-3 hours per week which does not represent a large commitment of their time and can be spent in a flexible manner, suited to the needs of individual members. When averaged to 1.5 hours per week it represents a potential of 60 hours of PD per calendar year, which exceeds the requirements of the majority of PD quotas. Considering that the teachers involved in these online communities join voluntarily, it would indicate that they place a high value and worth on this participation (see Table 4.14). It also demonstrated that they are already engaging in long-term, embedded, ongoing PD.

A key finding of the study found that the majority of respondents (86.73%) agreed that participation in an online community represented meaningful PD. When asked if they could identify any advantages of participating in online communities, it was commonly raised by respondents that the freedom of being able to access PD in their own time, the convenience, the lack time pressures or structures to follow and that it was flexible were attractive.

Table 6.9

Coded messages from community transcript analysis that support research findings.

Key research findings for Professional Development	Coded messages from community transcript analysis that support research findings	No. of messages per code
		(N=546)
There is a demand for authentic and contextualised PD (Lloyd & Cochrane, 2006)	E1 Recognising the problem	37
	E2 Sense of puzzlement	64
	I3 Information exchange	17
	T4 Creating solutions	102
	C1 Vicarious application to the real world	30
	C2 Testing solutions	12
	C3 Defending solutions	12
Learning for teachers should be conducted collaboratively (Boyle et al., 2004; Goldenberg & Gallimore, 1991)	E1 Recognising the problem	37
	E2 Sense of puzzlement	64
	I3 Information exchange	17

	I4 Suggestions for consideration	32
	I5 Brainstorming	15
	T1 Convergence – among group members	74
	T2 Convergence – within a single message	32
	T3 Connecting ideas, synthesis	62
	T4 Creating solutions	102
Adult learners are internally motivated, self-directed and experienced (Knowles et al., 1998; Lee, 1998).	E1 Recognising the problem	37
	E2 Sense of puzzlement	64
	T1 Convergence – among group members	74
	T2 Convergence – within a single message	32
	T3 Connecting ideas, synthesis	62
	T4 Creating solutions	102
	C1 Vicarious application to the real world	30
	C2 Testing solutions	12
	C3 Defending solutions	12
Online communities provide flexibility of time and location (Hodkinson & Hodkinson, 2003).	All messages demonstrate this finding as evidenced by the asynchronous nature of the mode of communication. Messages are sent and responded to at different times and locations.	546

Evidence found in focus group forum

The focus group forum were asked if membership to an online professional community represented a worthwhile form of professional development. This was a critical question, as this study concerns itself with determining if such a membership has a role to play in the PD of teachers. It was hoped that the respondents would agree and provide reasons that were supported by the literature. This question generated 14 postings and the majority of respondents agreed that it represented a worthwhile form of professional development.

Membership to an online community would appear to satisfy the criteria that PD needs to be authentic and embedded in schools, as the following postings demonstrate:

- "It is a worthwhile PD activity because you are able to initiate topics which are of interest/concern to you when you most need help" (PD:4)

- "Just in time models are very powerful for the individual that is the focus of attention" (PD:5)
- "It's also often a just-in-time model of PD, rather than what is so often the case for real PD course, a just-in-case model" (PD:7)

This form of PD was also seen to be free from content restraints and had the ability to change and diversify according to members needs, as one respondent concluded

- "Maybe they are not as specific and directed as face-to-face PD, but I find them more diverse in scope, more consistent in delivery, and more effective over time" (PD:7)

The flexibility in time and location were commonly mentioned. With regard to this flexibility being able to be sustained over a longer period of time, one posting stated:

- "I think online communities are a great idea for PD because teachers can learn so much from each other yet we don't always have the time to visit other schools or talk to each other to share ideas. In find online communities very useful for this purpose because of their asynchronous nature – you can take part when it suits you which makes it easier to find the time." (PD:14)

One problem associated with membership to online communities was raised by two members of the forum and generated a consensus from the remaining respondents, the issue of how to prove time spent engaged in this form of PD. As one respondent asked:

- "So we all seem to agree it is a worthwhile form of PD, but how do we prove that to the bean counters? Do we provide them with logs, showing the time we spend on them so it can be counted as PD? They will want proof of participation before they relinquish control of PD into our hands..." (PD:15)

It is apparent from the results of the survey and transcript analysis that membership to an online community provides teachers with opportunities for authentic and relevant PD. It was shown that the types of learning activities that the online communities engage in are more suited to the specific characteristics of adult learners. A further advantage of this form of PD was the flexibility it offers with regard to time. The clearest indication that this form of PD is suitable for teachers emerged from the survey when 86.73% of respondents agreed that membership equalled meaningful PD.

7. Discussion and Conclusion

Discussion

This chapter will concern itself with discussing the findings presented in this study, based on data collected by an electronic survey, community transcript analysis and an electronic focus-group forum in relation to current research. These findings now need to be re-examined in relation to the aims of the study. The specific aim of the study was:

> To investigate online communities of practice as a source of continuous professional development for teachers.

The corollary aims guiding this study were:

1. To explore the self-sustaining and generative characteristics of online communities
2. To examine the building of relationships through professional communication
3. The impact of membership on teacher practice.

1. To investigate online communities of practice as a source of continuous professional development for teachers

The teaching profession is in a constant state of change (Gallimore, Dalton & Tharp, 1986) as new ideas and knowledge are disseminated amongst teachers. It has been suggested that there is a need for an ongoing, continuous form of PD (Richardson, 1992) to meet these changes. The uninterrupted nature of online communities present as a source of ongoing, continuous PD for teachers. Whilst long-term PD (over 6 months) was not a popular choice by respondents to the survey, four did identify that continuous and ongoing PD would be the most beneficial model. However, it was evident that members of online communities were in fact engaged in continuous, ongoing PD. The average length of membership was three years and as noted in the survey results, membership requires a commitment of time and if considered unworthy, it would not have continued for so long. If this is measured in context with the types of activities members participate in, the impact on teaching practices and the professional communication they engage in it can be concluded that membership represents a continuous form of PD. The focus-group forum was able to summarise the ongoing, continuous aspect by suggesting that the online community played an important role as a resource that was able to accommodate the constant need to change faced by teachers.

It is important to note that the respondents to the survey agreed that participation in an online community represented meaningful PD. This was clarified further by the focus-group forum, where it was suggested that PD needed to be authentic and embedded in schools. It was also stated that online communities were free from content restraints and were able to change and diversify according to members needs, thus providing access to continuous relevant PD.

2. To explore the self-sustaining and generative characteristics of online communities
It would appear that online communities are self-sustaining and generative. This was evident by the total number of messages coded in the transcript analysis (N=546). All four descriptors were present in the transcript analysis results, indicating the sustainability of the community activities (see Table 6.7). All four phases of the practical inquiry model (Garrison et al., 2001) were evident as the community discussions moved from triggering to resolution stages contextualised in both the real and virtual worlds.

The self-sustaining and generative nature of online communities was clearer when the community discussions were graphically presented. The most complex, bonded clusters clearly showed how community discussions were continued across longer periods of time (more than two weeks) and were able to absorb new trigger messages, divergent issues, multiple manifestations of inquisitive and tentative messages and not reach a resolution. Bonded clusters were clearly evident of self-sustaining, generative community activity (see Figure 5.7).

A key reason why online communities can be self-sustaining and generative lies in their authenticity and relevancy. As the survey concluded, teachers are looking for PD that is personally relevant, authentic and contextualised. This desire for authenticity was also evident in the transcript analysis (see Table 6.9) and continued to be a theme that arose throughout the data collection phase. Related to the need for PD to be authentic, was the desire for PD content to be decided by teachers and the content of community discussions is decided by members, hence ensuring relevancy and authenticity. This would also ensure that membership and participation was able to be sustained.

Associated to self-sustainability is flexibility. Teachers are constrained by time and the majority of PD are conducted at the workplace after school or during vacation time (see Table 4.7). The ability for members to choose a time and location that is suitable for them helps in the self-sustainability of the community. A dynamic membership base would mean different members would be able to participate at different times and thus community activities continue to be generated. The survey found that on average, members spend 1.5 hours per week on community activities and when combined with the average three years they have maintained their membership presented evidence of the self-sustaining nature of membership to an online community.

3. To examine the building of relationships through professional communication
Membership to an online community can help in the building and maintaining of professional relationships (Hawkes, 1999). The relationships are not constrained by location, subject area, experience or background and are characteristically more global. The 'global' characteristic of this type of professional communication has an impact on pedagogical practice and PD. The composition of the online communities were clearly portrayed by the results from the survey, where it was shown that members displayed a variety of backgrounds and experience and represented a reliable cross-section of teaching professionals (see Table 4.2-3). The impact of this exposure on members was explained by the survey, where the ability to network and to receive emotional support were identified. It was also evidenced by the transcript analysis, as the total number of messages ($N=546$) shows the existence of relationships between members of the community because without relationships there would be no need for messages to be sent and received. Further evidence of the value members placed on building relationships was shown in the messages posted to the focus-group forum, where the majority commented on the relationships they formed and how they had moved across to the real-world.

Relationships between members are influenced by the stages of membership suggested by Lave and Wenger (1991). This was evidenced by the results from the transcript analysis (see Table 6.4) and from the forum, where it was clear that the level of membership influenced an individuals' level of learning and participation. As a member became more confident and experienced, their level of activity increased. A further influence on the building of relationships was the topic being discussed by the community. As the survey demonstrated, members actively participated in topics that were personally relevant or one which they felt they had the expertise to participate.

CMC has provided learners with a new context for professional communication that removes physical limitations and has created a new domain for learning. This new context for learning has been positively embraced by teachers as demonstrated by the number of memberships they hold and the length of time they have continued to hold them. This was further supported by the number of trigger messages coded from transcripts ($n=118$) which showed members initiating communication with their community (see Table 6.8). An insight into the nature of the relationships being established was provided by the survey, as it was discovered that the majority of members had over 20years of teaching experience and were thus seeking to improve or change their pedagogical practices.

Engaging in professional communication online provided teachers with opportunities to express their ideas and respond to other members messages. This was identified by respondents in the survey as being of great importance and was further supported by the transcript analysis (see Table 6.8). The ability to form relationships with peers enabled them to participate in professional discussion and this was identified by the messages posted in the focus-group forum. The value of building relationships via professional communication was evidenced by the findings of all three types of data collected and collectively they create a clear impression of the value members place on those relationships. The data shows that the members have an apparent understanding of the benefits of such a form of professional communication.

4. The impact of membership on teacher practice

Teachers are seeking changes to their practices that will result in positive change to student learning. Online communities provide teachers with the opportunity to discuss change, gather evidence of the effectiveness of changes (Galland, 2002) and provide teachers with feedback that will effect change more readily. The importance placed on this was evident in the survey when respondents ranked changing teaching practices first and improving student learning second regarding the aims of PD. The impact of membership on teaching practice was further demonstrated by the high priority teachers placed on acquiring practical skills that positively impacted on the classroom , as identified by the survey and the transcripts (see Figure 6.1).

Online communities appear to encourage the development of the expertise of a community which in turn helps to create peer-led practical learning activities. It was suggested that teachers were unwilling to implement changes suggested by outside experts, but desired to learn from peers in a participatory manner (see Table 4.6). The effectiveness of this form of learning was evident by the results from the focus-group forum, where respondents provided examples of how the community had impacted on their classrooms.

Not only are teachers seeking practical skills that have a positive effect on student learning, but they are seeking to accommodate constant changes to pedagogy (Richardson, 1992) and the need to absorb new skills and knowledge. It has been presented that the majority of teachers are working under a PD quota system but that this is failing to meet their needs. It was shown by the survey that many teachers went outside of this quota and sought extra PD and it was concluded that there were high levels of professionalism among teachers. This conclusion was further supported by evidence from the transcript analysis (see Table 6.5) where it can be seen that the majority of messages within the community were concerned with acquiring knowledge or solving problems.

It was popularly cited that members saw the online community fulfilling a PD role and this was provided as a reason for maintaining membership. It was seen as an opportunity to learn from peers and there was a growing understanding of their expertise and that of the community. The potential affect this had on teaching practices can be seen in the number of messages from the transcript analysis that demonstrated collaboration with peers (see Table 6.5). Evidently members are engaging in opportunities to learn, share and engage in professional discussion with their peers. These opportunities were identified as being critical for teachers in remote locations who could not maintain their professional learning. Further, the survey also showed that the immediacy and relevancy of responses had an influential impact on teaching practices.

Access to an online community results in self-regulated learning (see Table 6.5). Teachers responding to a trigger could quickly seek a solution, which resulted in changes to practices. This was supported by the survey where respondents provided examples to support this idea. The focus-group forum also supported the idea that teaching practices were constantly adjusting to change and that membership had been able to accommodate this need to change. Many changes are the result of encountering problems, and the ability of the online community to act as a problem solving resource was clear. There were 227 messages identified from the transcript analysis that demonstrated this ability (see Table 6.6) and the focus-group forum provided evidence supporting this idea.

The impact of membership on teaching practice is complex. It acts as forum for teachers to seek feedback on the potential of change to effect positive student learning outcomes and as a resource for solving problems they encounter. It helps teachers to develop a sense of expertise as they participate in peer-led learning and a high sense of professionalism. They provide the means for teachers to accommodate the constant need for change and respond to the self-regulatory instincts of teachers as they react to external and classroom-based triggers for change.

Conclusion

To conclude, it has been shown that online communities of practice are a valuable source of continuous professional development for teachers. They have the ability to provide support as teachers accommodate the constant changes and the need to acquire new skills and knowledge. The strength of this method of PD lies in its ability to be self-sustaining and generative. Teachers have access to authentic, relevant and flexible learning that is not constrained by time and can be accessed according to members needs. Online communities facilitate the building of relationships and encourage professional communication among peers. Membership to online communities has been shown to have a result in changes to teaching practices that result in positive change in student learning. It also has been shown to help develop professionalism among teachers and has helped to establish the expertise of the community as a resource for teachers. The participants in the study reached the conclusion that membership to online communities represents meaningful PD and it is now apparent that there is a wealth of evidence that supports this conclusion. It can be concluded that membership to online communities of practice represents a meaningful, relevant and authentic for of continuous professional development that is both well-used by a cross-section of teaching professionals and is thus highly applicable to a wider-section of teachers.

Appendix 1.

Collection 1 survey for members of the three nominated online communities involved in the study.

Faculty of Education
Queensland University of Technology

Online communities and professional development survey

This survey is aimed at helping us to understand why teachers join online communities, their experiences and their feelings about this form of online learning. It will be used as part of a larger study aimed at determining if membership to an online community represents a worthwhile form of professional development for teachers.

The survey is organised into the following sections:

a.   Background
b.   Professional Development
c.   The Online Community
d.   The use of Information and Communication technologies (ICTs)

It is hoped that the survey will provide a rich profile of the types of teachers who are members of professional online communities, their PD experiences and expectations, their impression of the online community and their use of ITCs.

By completing and returning this survey, you consent to participate in this research activity.

Start survey

Online communities and professional development survey

This electronic survey will be used in a study conducted as part of a Doctor of Philosophy program. The study is examining the possible role of online communities in the professional development of teachers.

Thank you for taking the time to participate in the study, your assistance is appreciated. Please take the time to read and answer the following questions.

Just a few points about this process:

- All responses are completely confidential.
- The survey will need to be completed in one session.
- The survey will take approximately 10-20 minutes.
- The survey is open until Friday 16th June, 2006.
- All respondents will remain anonymous

For further information about the questionnaire please contact Jennifer Duncan-Howell, on 07 3864 3646, email: j.duncanhowell@qut.edu.au.

A. Background

1. Gender

☐ Male

☐ Female

2. Age

☐ 20-29

☐ 30-39

☐ 40-49

☐ 50-59

☐ 60+

167

3. Please select the area you *currently* work in.

☐ Early Childhood

☐ Primary

☐ Secondary

☐ Tertiary

☐ Adult/Vocational

☐ Teacher Librarian

Other: [＿＿＿＿＿＿＿＿＿＿＿＿＿＿＿＿＿]

4. How many years teaching experience do you have?

☐ 1-5 years

☐ 6-10 years

☐ 11-15 years

☐ 16-20 years

☐ 20+ years

5. Please indicate your level of confidence in using ICTs.				
Very Poor	Poor	Competent	Highly competent	Professionally competent
☐	☐	☐	☐	☐

B. Professional Development (PD)

6. During the last 12 months, what types of PD have you experienced? Has any particular program left a favourable impression? If so, why?

7. Please comment on your PD requirements per year. You might like to comment on attendance (is it compulsory or voluntary), quotas that need to be reached (for example, a minimum number of hours) and your impression of the current PD system (positive or negative and why?).

8. Who in your opinion, would be the most appropriate to decide on the content of PD programs? Please select more than one if applicable.

☐ School Administration

☐ Education Authorities

☐ Department Heads

☐ Teaching staff

Other: [＿＿＿＿＿＿＿＿＿＿＿＿＿＿＿＿＿＿＿＿＿＿]

9. In your opinion, what method of learning do you best respond to?

☐ Learning with a group of colleagues face-to-face from your workplace.

☐ Learning with a group of colleagues face-to-face not from your workplace.

☐ Learning with a group of colleagues from your workplace electronically.

☐ Learning with an anonymous group of colleagues electronically

☐ Learning individually, in a course conducted away from your workplace.

☐ Learning individually and electronically.

Other: ⌐

10. Ideally, in your opinion, where should PD be conducted?

☐ At school / workplace

☐ At a higher education provider (e.g. University, Technical College)

☐ In a neutral environment (e.g. convention room)

☐ At home via the Internet

Other: ⌐

11. For real change to teaching practices, what duration should PD be?

☐ Short single sessions (1-2 hours)

☐ Short programs (e.g. 2-3 months)

☐ Longer programs (e.g. 6 months+)

Other: ⌐

12. What should be the aim of a PD program/session? Please rank the following statements, starting with 1 as the most important.

⌐ An improvement in student learning.

⌐ Positive change to teaching practices.

⌐ Obtaining new skills or knowledge.

⌐ Updating theoretical knowledge.

⌐ Solving problems encountered in the classroom.

⌐ Increasing teacher motivation and enthusiasm.

⌐ Forging closer bonds with colleagues.

⌐ Creating a supportive learning environment within the workplace.

C. The online community

13. How many online communities do you belong to? These may include both professional and personal interest communities.

☐ just this one

☐ 1-3

☐ 4-6

☐ 7-10

☐ 10+

14. How long have you been a member of this online community

☐ less than 1 year

☐ 1-3 years

☐ 4-6 years

☐ 7-10 years

☐ 10+ years

15. How did you find this online community?

☐ Via a search engine

☐ Recommendation from a friend/colleague

☐ Via a link from a professional website

☐ As a requirement for further study (e.g. Postgraduate course)

Other: ⌐

16. What is the average amount of time per week spent participating in the online community? For example; reading emails, replying to discussion threads or other activities found on the website.

☐ less than 1 hour

☐ 1-3 hours

☐ 4-6 hours

☐ 7-10 hours

☐ 10+ hours

17. What keeps you as a member of this online community?

18. Has membership to the online community met your expectations?

19. Please select the statement that best describes your participation in the online community.

☐ My participation fluctuates, I go through periods of high participation to low participation according to outside pressures.

☐ My participation depends on the topic being discussed by the list, I participate more if I am interested in the topic.

☐ My participation depends on my needs. If I need help or advice then I am active, otherwise I do not participate.

☐ My participation is not limited to my own needs, I try to participate in most discussions.

20. Do you consider participation in the online community as a meaningful form of PD and would you recommend it to others in your field? Why?

174

21. Have you changed any of your teaching practices as a result of participating in the online community? If possible, please give an example.

22. Can you identify any advantages of participating in online communities as a form of PD?

23. Can you identify any disadvantages of participating in online communities as a form of PD?

177

24. Have any of the discussion threads you have read or participated in, been particularly memorable? If so, could you please explain why.

25. How did you learn your ICT skills?

179

26. How has ICT impacted on your work?

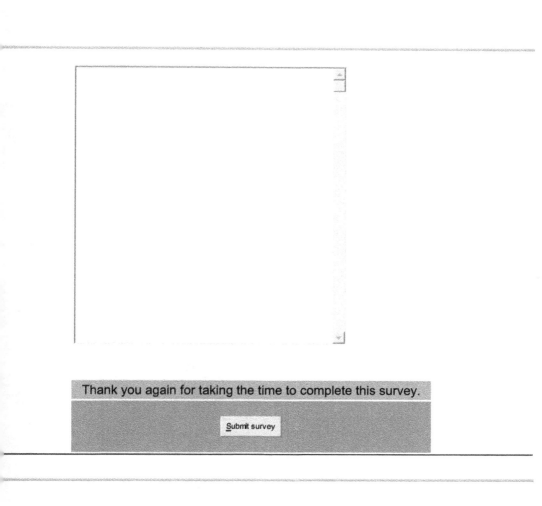

Thank you again for taking the time to complete this survey.

Submit survey

181

Appendix 2.

Forum Questions

1. Do you feel membership, to an online professional community represents a worthwhile form of professional development?

2. Is the on-going continuous nature of online communities an advantage? Why?

3. Have you used any ideas from the community discussions or activities in your classroom?

4. Have your teaching practices changed as a result from what you have learnt in the community?

5. How would you describe your initial presence in the community? Did you feel you were an outsider sitting on the edge observing? How did this change? What changed it?

6. Have you formed closer personal relationships with any members? For example, are there any members you met online via the community whom you now communicate personally with, either by email, telephone or face-to-face?

7. Do you use the online community as a problem solving resource? If so, has it been useful? Do you consider this to be an important role?

8. In your opinion, is professional discussion valuable? How is participating in professional discussion online different or better than professional discourse in your workplace?

Appendix 3.

Overview of coding of Community Transcripts.

Community Transcript: BECTA - Top Teachers Jan2006, OzTeachers Jan2006, SSABSA Jan2006		
	Total No. of messages per Descriptor	Total No. of messages per Indicator
Evocative (Triggering event)	128	
E1 Recognising the problem		62
E2 Sense of puzzlement		64
Inquisitive (Exploration)	153	
I1 – Divergence – within the online community		37
I2 Divergence – within a single message		15
I3 Information exchange		15
I4 Suggestions for consideration		40
I5 Brainstorming		17
I6 Leaps to conclusions		29
Tentative (Integration)	378	
T1 Convergence – among group members		108
T2 Convergence – within a single message		40
T3 Connecting ideas, synthesis		17
T4 Creating solutions		29
Committed (Resolution)	64	
C1 Vicarious application to real world		37

C2 Testing solutions		14
C3 Defending solutions		13
Total No. of messages coded	723	723

References

Abdal-Haqq, I. (1996). Making time for teacher professional development. *ERIC Digest, ED400259.*

ABS. (2003). *Australian Social Trends, 2003.* Canberra, ACT.

ABS. (2005). *Schools, Australia 2005.* Canberra, ACT.

ACOT. (1996). *Changing the conversation about teaching, learning and technology: A report on 10 years of ACOT research.*

Anderson, J. R., Reder, L. M., & Simon, H. A. (1996). Situated learning and education. *Educational Researcher, 25*(4), 5-11.

Anderson, J. R., Reder, L. M., & Simon, H. A. (1997). Situative versus cognitive perspectives: Form versus substance. *Educational Researcher, 26*(1), 18-21.

Babbie, E. (1990). *Survey Research Methods.* Belmont, California: Wadsworth Publishing Company.

Bales, R. F. (1951). *Interaction Process Analysis.* Cambridge, Mass.: Addison-Wesley Press, INC.

Bales, R. F. (1973). The equilibrium problems in small groups. In M. Argyle (Ed.), *Social Encounters: Readings in social interactions* (pp. 221-236). Chicago: Aldine Publishing Company.

Bales, R. F. (1999). *Social Interaction Systems: Theory and measurement.* New Brunswick: Transaction Publishers.

Barab, S. A., MacKinster, J. G., Moore, J. A., Cunningham, D. J., & team, T. I. D. (2001). Designing and building an online community: The struggle to support sociability in the inquiry learning forum. *Educational Technology Research and Development, 49*(4), 1042-1629.

Barnett, R. (1999). Learning to work and working to learn. In D. Boud & J. Garrick (Eds.), *Understanding learning at work.* (pp. 29-44). London: Routledge.

Beams, S. (2004). *Towards a model of effective professional development for teachers of ICT.* Unpublished Masters, Queensland University of Technology, Brisbane.

Bean, W. (2004). Teacher learning and the role of school culture. *Literacy learning in the middle years., 12*(2), 61-68.

Becker, H. J. (1993). Instructional computer use: Findings from a national survey of school and teacher practices. *The Computing Teacher, 20*(7), 6-7.

Billet, S. (1993). *Learning is working when working is learning - a guide to learning in the workplace.* Brisbane: The Centre for Skill Formation Research and Development, Griffith University.

Billet, S. (2001). *Learning in the workplace: Strategies for effective practice.* Sydney: Allen & Unwin.

Billet, S. (2001). Learning throughout working life: Interdependencies at work. *Studies in Continuing Education, 23*(1), 19-35.

Boardman, A. G., & Woodruff, A. L. (2004). Teacher change and "high stakes" assessment: what happens to professional development? *Teaching and Teacher Education, 20,* 545-557.

Bonamy, J., & Haughluslaine-Charlier, B. (1995). Supporting professional learning: beyond technical support. *Journal of Computer Assisted Learning, 11*(4), 196-202.

Bond, P. (2004). Communities of Practice and complexity: conversation and culture. *Organisations and People, 11*(4), 1-7.

Borko, H., Mayfield, V., Marion, S., Flexer, R., & Cumbro, K. (1997). Teachers' developing ideas and practices about mathematics performance assessment: Successes, stumbling blocks and implications for professional development. *Teaching and Teacher Education, 13,* 259-278.

Borko, H., & Putnam, R. T. (1995). Expanding a teacher's knowledge base: a cognitive psychological

    perspective on professional development. In T. R. Guskey & M. Huberman (Eds.),

    Professional development in education: New paradigms and practices (pp. 35-65). New York:

    Teachers College Press.

Bowles, M. S. (2004). *Relearning to E-learn.* Melbourne: Melbourne University Press.

Boyle, B., While, D., & Boyle, T. (2004). A longitudinal study of teacher change: What makes

    professional development effective? *The Curriculum Journal, 15*(1), 45-68.

Bray, J. N. (2002). Uniting teacher learning: Collaborative inquiry for professional development. *New*

    Directions for Adult and Continuing Education, 94(Summer), 83-92.

Breitmayer, B. J., Ayres, L., & Knafl, A. (1993). Triangulation in Qualitative research: evaluation of

    completeness and confirmation purposes. *IMAGE: Journal of Nursing Scholarship, 25*(3), 237-

    243.

Bronack, S. C., Kilbane, C. R., Herbert, J. M., & McNergney, R. F. (1999). In-service and pre-service

    teachers' perceptions of a web-based, case-based learning environment. *Journal of*

    Information Technology for Teacher Education, 8(3), 305-320.

Brown, J. S., Collins, A., & Duguid, P. (1989). Situated cognition and the culture of learning.

    Educational Researcher, 18(1), 32-42.

Burley, H., Yearwood, B., Elwood-Salinas, S., Martin, L., & Allen, D. (2001). Partners in cyberspace:

    Reflections on developing an ePDS. *The Educational Forum, 65*(2), 166-175.

Candy, P. C. (1989). Alternative paradigms in educational research. *Australian Educational*

    Researcher, 16(3), 1-11.

Chen, T.-L., & Chen, T.-J. (2002). *A strategic analysis of the online learning community for continuing*

    professional development of university faculty in Taiwan: A SWOT analysis. Paper presented

187

at the International Conference on Computers in Education (ICCE'02).

Clouder, L., & Deepwell, F. (2004). *Reflections on unexpected outcomes: learning from student collaboration in an online discussion forum.* Paper presented at the Networked Learning Conference 2004, Sheffield, UK.

Coate, J. (1997). Cyberspace innkeeping: Building online community. In P. E. Agre & D. Schuler (Eds.), *Reinventing technology, rediscovering community: Critical explorations of computing as social practice.* (pp. 165-189). Greenwich, CT: Ablex.

Cobb, P. (1994). Where is the mind? Constructivist and sociocultural perspectives on mathematical development. *Educational Researcher, 23*(7), 13-19.

Cobb, P., & Bowers, J. S. (1999). Cognitive and situated learning perspectives in theory and practice. *Educational Researcher, 28*(2), 4-15.

Commonwealth Department of Education, S. a. T. (2001). *Making better connections: Models of teacher professional development for the integration of information and communication technology into classroom practice.* Canberra.

Connelly, F. M., & Clandinin, D. J. (1990). Stories of expertise and narrative inquiry. *Educational Researcher, 19*(5), 2-14.

Coomber, R. (1997). Using the Internet for survey research. *Sociological Research Online, 2*(2), 1-13.

Corich, S., Kinshuk, & Hunt, L. M. (2004). *Assessing discussion forum participation: in search of quality.* Retrieved 20th July, 2005, from http://www.itdl.org/Journal/Dec_04/article01.htm

Cornu, B. (2004). Networking and collecting intelligence for teachers and learners. In A. Brown & N. Davis (Eds.), *Digital Technology, Communities and Education* (pp. 40-45). London: Routledge Falmer.

Crandall, D. P. (1983). The teacher's role in school improvement. *Educational Leadership, 41*(3), 6-10.

Crawford, M. (2002). Enhancing School Leadership. *Educational Management and Administration, 30*(4), 431-445.

Creswell, J. W. (2005). *Educational Research* (Second ed.). Upper Saddle River, NJ: Pearson Education.

Darling-Hammond, L. (1995). Changing the conceptions of teaching and teacher development. *Teacher Education Quarterly, 22*(4), 9-26.

Day, C. (1999). *Teachers: The challenges of lifelong learning.* London: The Falmer Press.

Dewacht, P. (2004). Online collaborative mentoring. *EDUCARE News*(May), 8-11.

Dillman, D. A. (2000). *Mail and Internet Surveys: The Tailored Design Method.* New York: John Wiley & Sons, Inc.

Down, B., Chadbourne, R., & Hogan, C. (2000). How are teachers managing performance management? *Asia-Pacific Journal of Teacher Education, 28*(3), 213-223.

Doyle, W. (1990). Case methods in teacher education. *Teacher Education Quarterly, 17*(1), 7-15.

Driver, R., Asoko, H., Leach, J., Mortimer, E., & Scott, P. (1994). Constructing scientific knowledge in the classroom. *Educational Researcher, 23*(7), 5-12.

Eisenhardt, K. M. (1989). Building theories from case study research. *The academy of management review, 14*(4), 532-550.

Elmore, R. F., & Burney, D. (1999). Investing in teacher learning. In L. Darling-Hammond & G. Sykes (Eds.), *Teaching as the learning profession: Handbook of policy and practice.* (pp. 263-291). San Francisco: Jossey-Bass Publishers.

Engestrom, Y. (1999). Situated Learning at the threshold of the new millennium. In J. Bliss, R. Saljo &

P. Light (Eds.), *Learning sites: social and technological resources for learning* (pp. 249-258). Amsterdam: Pergamon.

England, J. T. (1992). *Building community for the 21st century*. Retrieved 11th June, 2004

Evans, K., & Rainbird, H. (2002). The significance of workplace learning for a 'learning society'. In K. Evans, P. Hodkinson & L. Unwin (Eds.), *Working to learn: Transforming learning in the workplace.* (pp. 7-28). London: Kogan Page.

Fowler, F. J. (1995). *Improving survey questions: Design and evaluation* (Vol. 38). Newbury Park: SAGE Publications.

Fowler, F. J., & Mangione, T. W. (1990). *Standardized Survey Interviewing: Minimizing interviewer-related error* (Vol. 18). Newbury Park: SAGE Publications.

Franke, M. L., Carpenter, T., Fennema, E., & Behrend, J. (1998). Understanding teachers' self-sustaining, generative change in the context of professional development. *Teaching and Teacher Education, 14*, 67-80.

Galland, P. (2002). Techie Teachers - web-based staff development at your leisure. *TechTrends, 46*(3), 11-16.

Gallimore, R., Dalton, S., & Tharp, R. G. (1986). Self-regulation and interactive teaching: The effects of teaching conditions on teachers' cognitive activity. *The Elementary School Journal, 86*(5), 613-631.

Garet, M. S., Porter, A. C., Desimone, L., Birman, B. F., & Yoon, K. S. (2001). What makes professional development effective? Results from a national sample of teachers. *American Educational Research Journal, 38*(4), 915-945.

Garrison, D. R., Anderson, T., & Archer, W. (2000). Critical Inquiry in a text-based environment: Computer conferencing in higher education. *The Internet and Higher Education, 2*(2-3), 87-

105.

Garrison, D. R., Anderson, T., & Archer, W. (2001). Critical thinking, cognitive presence, and computer conferencing in distance education. *The American Journal of Distance Education, 15*(1), 7-23.

Garvey, L. (2002). Flexible delivery of professional development in ICT. *QUICK, 86,* 8-15.

Gilbert, P. K., & Dabbagh, N. (2005). How to structure online discussions for meaningful discourse: a case study. *British Journal of Educational Technology, 36*(1), 5-18.

Goldberger, P. (2003). *Disconnected Urbanism.* Retrieved 28th June, 2005, from http://www.metropolismag.com/html/content_1103/obj/index.html

Goldenberg, C., & Gallimore, R. (1991). Changing teaching takes more than a one-shot workshop. *Educational Leadership, 49*(3), 69-72.

Goodyear, P., & Steeples, C. (1999). Asynchronous multimedia conferencing in continuing professional development: Issues in the representation of practice through user-created video-clips. *Distance Education, 20*(1), 31-48.

Gould Boardman, A., & Woodruff, A. L. (2004). Teacher change and "high stakes" assessment: what happens to professional development? *Teaching and Teacher Education, 20,* 545-557.

Grabowski, B., Pusch, S., & Pusch, W. (1990). Social and intellectual value of computer-mediated communications in a graduate community. *ETTI, 27*(3), 276-283.

Gray, B. (2004). Informal learning in an online community of practice. *Journal of Distance Education, 19*(1), 20-35.

Greeno, J. G. (1997). On claims that answer the wrong question. *Educational Researcher, 26*(1), 5-17.

Greeno, J. G. (1998). The situativity of knowing, learning and research. *American Psychologist, 53*(1),

191

5-26.

Gregson, K. (1999). *Online discussion groups: The potential for political participation.* Paper presented at the Annual meeting of the American Political Science Association 2-5th September 1999, Atlanta, GA.

Griffin, G. A. (1983). Implications of research for staff development programs. *The Elementary School Journal, 83*(4), 414-426.

Gunawardena, C. N., Lowe, C. A., & Anderson, T. (1997). Analysis of a global online debate and the development of an interaction analysis model for examining social construction of knowledge in computer conferencing. *Journal of Educational Computing Research, 17*(4), 397-431.

Gunawardena, C. N., Lowe, C. A., & Anderson, T. (1998). *Transcript analysis of computer-mediated conferences as a tool for testing constructivist and social-constructivist learning theories.* Paper presented at the Distance Learning Conference 1998, Madison, WI.

Gundry, J. (1992). Understanding collaborative learning in networked organisations. In A. R. Kaye (Ed.), *Collaborative learning through computer conferencing: The Najaden Papers* (pp. 167-178). Berlin: Springer-Verlag.

Guskey, T. R. (1985). Staff development and teacher change. *Educational Leadership, 42*(7), 56-60.

Guskey, T. R. (1986). Staff development and the process of teacher change. *Educational Researcher, 15*(5), 5-20.

Guskey, T. R. (2002). Professional development and teacher change. *Teachers and Teaching, 8*(3/4), 381-391.

Hammond, M. (2000). Communication within online forums: the opportunities, the constraints and the value of a communicative approach. *Computers and Education, 35*, 251-262.

Hara, N., Bonk, C. J., & Angeli, C. (2000). Content analysis of online discussion in an applied educational psychology. *Instructional Science, 28*(2), 115-152.

Harasim, L. M. (1990). Online Education: An environment for collaboration and intellectual amplification. In L. M. Harasim (Ed.), *Online Education: Perspectives on a new environment* (pp. 39-66). New York: Praeger.

Hargreaves, A. (1993). Individualism and individuality: Reinterpreting the teacher culture. In J. W. Little & M. W. McLaughlin (Eds.), *Teachers' work: Individuals, colleagues and context.* (pp. 51-75). New York: Teaches College Press.

Hase, S., & Kenyon, C. (2000). *From Andragogy to Heutagogy.* Retrieved August 12th, 2006, from http://ultibase.rmit.edu.au/Articles/dec00/hase2.htm

Havelock, B. (2004). Online community and professional learning in education: Research-based keys to sustainability. *Advancement of Computing in Education, 12*(1), 56-84.

Hawkes, M. (1999). Exploring network-based communication in teacher professional development. *Educational Technology, 39*(4), 45-52.

Hawley Orrill, C. (2001). Building technology-based, learner-centered classrooms: The evolution of a professional development framework. *Educational Technology Research and Development, 49*(1), 15-34.

Haythornthwaite, C. (2002). Building social networks via computer networks: Creating and sustaining distributed learning communities. In K. A. Renninger & W. Shumar (Eds.), *Building Virtual Communities: Learning and change in cyberspace* (pp. 159-190). Cambridge: Cambridge University Press.

Hedderson, J. (1991). *SPSS/PC+ Made Simple.* Belmont, California: Wadsworth Publishing Company.

Henri, F. (1992). Computer conferencing and content analysis. In A. R. Kaye (Ed.), *Collaborative*

193

learning through computer conferencing: The Najaden Papers (pp. 117-136). Berlin: Springer-Verlag.

Henri, F., & Pudelko, B. (2003). Understanding and analysing activity and learning in virtual communities. *Journal of Computer Assisted Learning, 19*, 474-487.

Hiltz, S. R. (1990). Evaluating the virtual classroom. In L. M. Harasim (Ed.), *Online Education: Perspectives on a new environment* (pp. 133-184). New York: Praeger.

Hiltz, S. R. (1998). *Collaborative learning in asynchronous learning networks: Building learning communities.* Paper presented at the WebNet 98 World Conference of the WWW, Orlando, FL.

Hoadley, C., & Pea, R. D. (2002). Finding the ties that bind: Tools in support of a knowledge-building community. In K. A. Renninger & W. Shumar (Eds.), *Building Virtual Communities: Learning and change in cyberspace* (pp. 321-354). Cambridge: Cambridge University Press.

Hoban, G., & Herrington, T. Attempting to keep the conversation going: Exploring the use of a web-based environment to support teachers' action learning.

Hodkinson, P., & Bloomer, M. (2002). Learning careers: Conceptualising lifelong work-based learning. In K. Evans, P. Hodkinson & L. Unwin (Eds.), *Working to learn: Transforming learning in the workplace.* (pp. 29-43). London: Kogan Page.

Hodkinson, P., & Hodkinson, H. (2003). Individuals, Communities of Practice and the policy context: School teachers' learning in their workplace. *Studies in Continuing Education, 25*(1), 3-21.

Hoffman, E., & Thompson, G. (2000). Putting the research to work. *TechTrends, 44*(2), 20-23.

Hord, S. M. (1997). Professional Learning Communities: What are they and why are they important? *SEDL: Issues.....about Change, 6*(1), 1-10.

Houle, C. (1950). *Patterns of learning.* San Francisco: Jossey-Bass.

Howell-Richardson, C., & Mellar, H. (1996). A methodology for the analysis of patterns of
    participation within computer mediated communication courses. *Instructional Science, 24,*
    47-69.

Huberman, M. (1995). Professional careers and professional development: Some intersections. In T.
    R. Guskey & M. Huberman (Eds.), *Professional development in education: New paradigms
    and practices.* (pp. 192-224). New York: Teachers College Press.

Huberman, M. (2001). Networks that alter teaching: Conceptualisations, exchanges and
    experiments. In J. Soler, A. Craft & H. Burgess (Eds.), *Teacher Development: Exploring our
    own practice.* (pp. 141-159). London: Paul Chapman Publishing Ltd.

Hummel, J. (2002). *Social profiles of virtual communities.* Paper presented at the 35th International
    Conference on System Sciences, Hawaii.

Hung, D. W. L., & Chen, D. (2001). Situated cognition, Vygotskian thought and learning from the
    Communities of Practice perspective: Implications for the design of web-based e-learning.
    Education Media International, 38(1), 3-12.

Hunter, B. (2002). Learning in the virtual community depends upon changes in local communities. In
    K. A. Renninger & W. Shumar (Eds.), *Building Virtual Communities* (pp. 96-126). Cambridge:
    Cambridge University Press.

Ingvarson, L., Meiers, M., & Beavis, A. (2003). *Evaluating the quality and impact of professional
    development programs.* Paper presented at the ACER Research Conference.

Jacob, E. (1987). Qualitative research traditions: A review. *Review of Educational Research, 57*(1), 1-
    50.

Jenson, J., Lewis, B., & Smith, R. (2002). No one way: Working models for teachers' professional development. *Journal of Technology and Teacher Education, 10*(4), 481-496.

Johansson, R. (2003). *Case study methodology reflected in Architectural Research.* Retrieved 12th

December, 2006, from http://www.infra.kth.se/~rolfj/Foufaces2003.pdf

Kaufman, H. F. (1959). Toward an interactional conception of community. *Social Forces, 38*(1), 8-17.

Kelle, U., & Laurie, H. (1995). Computer use in qualitative research and issues of validity. In U. Kelle

(Ed.), *Computer-aided qualitative data analysis: Theory, methods and practice* (pp. 19-28).

London: Sage Publications.

Kemmis, S. (1989). Critical reflection. In M. F. Wideen & I. Andrews (Eds.), *Staff development for*

school improvement: A focus on the teacher. (pp. 73-90). New York: The Falmer Press.

Kiesler, S. (1992). Talking, teaching, and learning in networked groups: Lessons from research. In A.

R. Kaye (Ed.), *Collaborative learning through computer conferencing: The Najaden Papers*

(pp. 147-166). Berlin: Springer-Verlag.

King, K. P., & Wright, L. (2003). New perspectives on gains in the ABE classroom: Transformational

learning results considered. *Adult Basic Education, 13*(2), 100-112.

Knowles, M., Holton, E. F., & Swanson, R. A. (1998). *The Adult Learner* (Fifth Edition ed.). Houston:

Gulf Publishing Company.

Krauss, R. M., & Fussell, S. R. (1991). Constructing shared communicative environments. In L. B.

Resnick, J. M. Levine & S. D. Teasley (Eds.), *Perspectives on socially shared cognition.* (pp.

172-202). Washington: American Psychological Association.

Krosnick, J. A. (1999). Survey Research. *Annual Review of Psychology, 50,* 537-567.

Kuehn, S. A. (1994). Computer-mediated communication in instructional settings: a research agenda.

Communication Education, 43, 171-183.

Lajoie, S. P. (1993). Computer environments as cognitive tools for enhancing learning. In S. P. Lajoie
      & S. J. Derry (Eds.), *Computers as cognitive tools* (pp. 261-288). Hillsdale, New Jersey:
      Lawrence Erlbaum Associates.

Lampert, M. (1997). Teaching about thinking and thinking about teaching, revisited. In V. Richardson
      (Ed.), *Constructivist teacher education: Building new understandings.* (pp. 84-107). London:
      The Falmer Press.

Lasker, J. N., Sogolow, E. D., & Sharim, R. R. (2005). The role of an online community for people with
      a rare disease: content analysis of messages posted on a primary biliary cirrhosis mailing list.
      Journal of Medical Internet Research, 7(1), e10.

Lave, J. (1988). *Cognition in practice.* Cambridge: Cambridge University Press.

Lave, J. (1991). Situated learning in Communities of Practice. In L. B. Resnick, J. M. Levine & S. D.
      Teasley (Eds.), *Perspectives on socially shared cognition* (pp. 63-84). Washington: American
      Psychological Association.

Lave, J., & Wenger, E. (1991). *Situated learning: Legitimate peripheral participation.* Cambridge:
      Cambridge University Press.

Lawley, E. L. (1994). *The sociology of culture in computer-mediated communication: An initial
      exploration.* Retrieved 28th June, 2005, from http://www.itcs.com/elawley/bourdieu.html

Leask, M., & Younie, S. (2001). Building on-line communities for teachers: issues emerging from
      research. In M. Leask (Ed.), *Issues in teaching using ICT* (pp. 223-232). London: Routledge
      Falmer.

Lechner, S. (1998). Teachers of the N-Gen need reflective online communities. *Journal of Online
      Learning, 9*(3), 20-24.

Lee, C. (1998). The adult learner: neglected no more. *Training, 35*(3), 47-52.

Lee, S. W. (2003). *Software evaluation research: Case study methodology designed research.* Retrieved 11th December 2006, from http://www.sis.uncc.edu/~seoklee/Projects/CSM.htm

Leimeister, J. M., Sidiras, P., & Kremar, H. (2004). *Success factors of virtual communities from the perspective of members and operators: An empirical study.* Paper presented at the 37th International Conference on System Sciences.

Levin, J. A., Kim, H., & Riel, M. (1990). Analyzing instructional interactions on electronic message networks. In L. M. Harasim (Ed.), *Online Education: Perspectives on a new environment* (pp. 185-214). New York: Praeger.

Levinson, P. (1990). Computer conferencing in the context of the evolution of media. In L. M. Harasim (Ed.), *Online Education: Perspectives on a new environment* (pp. 3-14). New York: Praeger.

Levy, P. (1999). AN example of Internet-based continuing professional development: perspectives on course design and participation. *Education for Information, 17*, 45-58.

Levy, P. (2003). A methodological framework for practice-based research in networked learning. *Instructional Science, 31*, 87-109.

Li, Q. (2004). Knowledge building community: Keys for using online forums. *TechTrends, 48*(4), 24-28.

Lindeman, E. (1926). *The meaning of adult education.* New York: New Republic.

Lloyd, M. (2000). Reinventing Practice: the Second Year. *QUICK, 78*, 22-25.

Lloyd, M. (2001). Reinventing Practice: the Second Year. *QUICK, 81*, 16-19.

Lloyd, M., & Cochrane, J. (2006). *Celtic knots: Interweaving the elements of effective teacher professional development in ICT.* Paper presented at the ACEC 2006 National Conference,, Cairns, QLD.

Lloyd, M., & McRobbie, C. (2005). The "Whole Approach": An investigation of School-based

    practicum model of teacher professional development in ICT. *Educational Computing*

    Research, 32(4), 341-353.

London, M., & Smither, J. W. (1999). Empowered self-development and continuous learning. *Human*

    Resources Management, 38(1), 3-15.

Lowenberg Ball, D., & Cohen, D. K. (1999). Developing practice, developing practitioners. In L.

    Darling-Hammond & G. Sykes (Eds.), *Teaching as the learning profession: Handbook of policy*

    and practice. (pp. 3-32). San Francisco: Jossey-Bass Publishers.

Marx, R. W., Blumenfeld, P. C., & Krajcik, J. S. (1998). New technologies for teacher professional

    development. *Teaching and Teacher Education, 14*(1), 33-52.

Matei, S. A. (2005). *From counterculture to cyberculture: virtual community discourse and the*

    dilemma of modernity. Retrieved 10th August, 2005, from

    http://jcmc.indiana.edu/vol10/issue3/matei.html

Mayer, R. E. (2003). Elements of a science of e-learning. *Journal of Educational Computing Research,*

    29(3), 297-313.

McCreary, E. K. (1990). Three behavioural models for computer-mediated communication. In L. M.

    Harasim (Ed.), *Online Education: Perspectives on a new environment* (pp. 117-130). New

    York: Praeger.

McLaughlin, M. W. (1993). What matters most in teachers' workplace context? In J. W. Little & M.

    W. McLaughlin (Eds.), *Teachers' work: Individuals, colleagues and context.* (pp. 79-103). New

    York: Teachers College Press.

McLoughlin, C., & Luca, J. (1999). *Lonely outpourings or reasoned dialogue? An analysis of text-based*

    conferencing as a tool to support learning. Paper presented at the 1999 ASCILITE

Conference.

McNickle, C. (2003). *The impact that ICT has on how we learn - pedagogy, andragogy or heutagogy?* Paper presented at the 16th ODLAA Biennial Forum Conference Proceedings.

Mellar, H., & Kambouri, M. (2004). Learning and teaching adult basic skills with digital technology. In A. Brown & N. Davis (Eds.), *Digital technology, Communities and Education* (pp. 131-144). London: Routledge Falmer.

Merseth, K. K., & Lacey, C. A. (1993). Weaving stronger fabric: The pedagogical promise of hypermedia and case methods in teacher education. *Teaching and Teacher Education, 9*(3), 283-299.

Miles, M. B., & Huberman, A. M. (1994). *Qualitative Data Analysis* (Second ed.). Thousand Oaks: SAGE Publications.

Moore, J. A., & Barab, S. A. (2002). The Inquiry learning forum: a community of practice approach to online professional development. *TechTrends, 46*(3), 44-50.

Morrison, J. L. (1992). Environmental scanning. In M. A. Whitely, J. D. Porter & R. H. Fenske (Eds.), *A primer for new institutional researchers.* (pp. 86-99). Tallahassee, Florida: The Association for Institutional Research.

Mowrer, D. E. (1996). A content analysis of student/instructor communication via computer conferencing. *Higher Education, 32*, 217-241.

Murphy, K. L., & Collins, M. P. (1997). *Communication conventions in instructional electronic chats.* Retrieved 10th August, 2005, from http://www.firstmonday.dk/issues/issue2_11/murphy/index.html

Newman, D. R., Webb, B., & Cochrane, C. (1995). A content analysis method to measure critical thinking in face-to-face and computer supported group learning. *Interpersonal Computing* and Technology, 3(2), 56-77.

Nolan, D. J., & Weiss, J. (2002). Learning in cyberspace: an educational view of virtual community. In

    K. A. Renninger & W. Shumar (Eds.), *Building Virtual Communities: Learning and change in*

    cyberspace (pp. 293-320). Cambridge: Cambridge University Press.

Oliver, R., & Omari, A. (1999). Using online technologies to support problem-based learning:

    Learners' responses and perceptions. *Australian Journal of Educational Technology, 15*(1),

    58-79.

Ollila, M., & Simpson, A. (2004). *Dimensions of design: a comparison of professional development in*

    two online learning communities. Paper presented at the International Conference on

    Advanced Learning Technologies (ICALT'04).

Oriogun, P. K. (2003). Towards understanding online learning levels of engagement using SQUAD

    approach to CMC discourse. *Australian Journal of Educational Technology, 19*(3), 371-387.

Pachler, N. (2001). Connecting schools and pupils: to what end? Issues related to the use of ICT in

    school-based learning. In M. Leask (Ed.), *Issues in Teaching using ICT* (pp. 15-30). London:

    Routledge Falmer.

Papert, S. (1993). *The Children's Machine*. New York: Basic Books.

Paulus, T. M. (2005). Collaborative and Cooperative Approaches to Online Group Work: The impact

    of task type. *Distance Education, 26*(1), 111-125.

Phelps, R., & Graham, A. (2004). Teachers and ICT: Exploring a metacognitive approach to

    professional development. *Australasian Journal of Educational Technology, 20*(1), 49-68.

Porter, C. E. (2004). A typology of virtual communities: A multi-disciplinary foundation for future

    research. *Journal of Computer-Mediated Communication, 10*(1),

    http://jcmc.indiana.edu/vol10/issue11/porter.html.

Preece, J., & Maloney-Krichmar, D. (2005). Online Communities: Design, theory and practice. *Journal of Computer-Mediated Communication, 10*(4), http://jcmc.indiana.edu/vol10/issue14/preece.html.

Putnam, R. T., & Borko, H. (2000). What do new views of knowledge and thinking have to say about research on teacher learning? *Educational Researcher, 29*(1), 4-15.

Rachal, J. R. (2002). Andragogy's Detectives: A critique of the present and a proposal for the future. *Adult Education Quarterly, 52*(3), 210-227.

Rheingold, H. (2000). *The Virtual Community: Homesteading on the electronic frontier.* New York: Harper Perennial.

Richardson, V. (1990). Significant and worthwhile change in teaching practice. *Educational Researcher, 19*(7), 10-18.

Richardson, V. (1992). The agenda-setting dilemma in a constructivist staff development process. *Teaching and Teacher Education, 8*(3), 287-300.

Richardson, V. (1994). Conducting research on practice. *Educational Researcher, 23*(5), 5-10.

Richardson, V. (1997). Constructivist teaching and teacher education: Theory and practice. In V. Richardson (Ed.), *Constructivist teacher education: Building new understandings* (pp. 3-14). London: The Falmer Press.

Richardson, V., & Placier, P. (2001). Teacher change. In V. Richardson (Ed.), *Handbook of research on teaching.* (Fourth ed., pp. 905-947). Washington: American Educational Research Association.

Riel, M. (1996). *The Internet: A land to settle than an ocean to surf. A new place for school reform through community development.* Retrieved 21st February, 2005, from http://www.nekesc.k12.ks.us/usa/community.html

Rodriquez Illera, J. L. (2004). Multimedia learning in the digital world. In A. Brown & N. Davis (Eds.), *Digital Technology, Communities and Education* (pp. 46-56). London: Routledge Falmer.

Rogers, J. (2000). Communities of Practice: A framework for fostering coherence in virtual learning communities. *Educational Technology and Society, 3*(3), 1-12.

Ruberg, L. F., Moore, D. M., & Taylor, C. D. (1996). Student participation, interaction, and regulation in a computer-mediated communication environment: A qualitative study. *Journal of Educational Computing Research, 14*(3), 243-268.

Sacks, H. (1972). An initial investigation of the usability of conversational data for doing sociology. In D. Sudnow (Ed.), *Studies in social interaction* (pp. 31-74). New York: The Free Press.

Salmon, G. (2000). *E-Moderating: The key to teaching and learning online.* London: Kogan Page.

Salomon, G. (1991). Transcending the qualitative - quantitative debate: The analytic and systemic approaches to educational research. *Educational Researcher, 20*(6), 10-18.

Sapsford, R. (1999). *Survey Research.* London: SAGE Publications.

Schegloff, E. A. (1972). Notes on a conversational practice: formulating place. In D. Sudnow (Ed.), *Studies in Social Interaction* (pp. 75-119). New York: The Free Press.

Scardamalia, M. & Bereiter, C. (1994). Computer Support for Knowledge-Building Communities. *The Journal of The Learning Sciences, 3*(3), 265-283.

Schlager, M. S., Fusco, J., & Schank, P. (2002). Evolution of an online education community of practice. In K. A. Renninger & W. Shumar (Eds.), *Building Virtual Communities: Learning and change in cyberspace* (pp. 129-158). Cambridge: Cambridge University Press.

Schrum, L. (1999). Technology professional development for teachers. *Educational Technology Research and Development, 47*(4), 83-39.

Shannon, S. (2003). Adult learning and CME. *The Lancet, 361*(9353), 266-268.

Sharpe, R., & Bailey, P. (1999). Evaluation and design of technologies to meet learning outcomes. *Journal of Computer Assisted Learning, 15*(3), 179-188.

Sherif, M., & Sherif, C. W. (1973). Acceptable and unacceptable behaviour defined by group norms. In M. Argyle (Ed.), *Social Encounters: Readings in social interactions* (pp. 237-246). Chicago: Aldine Publishing Company.

Shulman, L. S., & Shulman, J. H. (2004). How and what teachers learn: A shifting perspective. *Journal of Curriculum Studies, 36*(2), 257-271.

Shultz, G., & Cuthbert, A. (2002). *Teacher professional development and online learning communities*. Retrieved 9th November, 2004, from http://kie.berkeley.edu/transitions/teacherPD.html

Smith, M. K. (2003). *The Encyclopaedia of Informal Education*. Retrieved 9th November, 2004, from http://www.infed.org/biblio/communities_of_practice.htm

Sorensen, E. K., & Takle, E. S. (2004). A cross-cultural cadence in E: Knowledge building with networked communities across disciplines and cultures. In A. Brown & N. Davis (Eds.), *Digital Technology, Communities and Education* (pp. 251-263). London: Routledge Falmer.

Sorge, D. H., & Russell, J. D. (2000). A strategy for effective change in instructional behaviour: Staff development that works. *Educational Technology, XL*(6), 46-49.

Speier, M. (1972). Some conversational problems for interactional analysis. In D. Sudnow (Ed.), *Studies in Social Interaction* (pp. 397-427). New York: The Free Press.

Stacey, E., Smith, P. J., & Barty, K. (2004). Adult learners in the workplace: Online learning and Communities of Practice. *Distance Education, 25*(1), 107-123.

Stake, R. E. (1978). The case study method in social inquiry. *Educational Researcher, 7*(2), 5-8.

Stake, R. E. (1995). *The art of case study research.* Thousand Oaks, CA: Sage.

Stake, R. E. (2003). Case Studies. In N. K. Denzin & Y. S. Lincoln (Eds.), *Strategies of Qualitative Inquiry* (pp. 134-164). London: SAGE Publications.

Stewart, D. W., & Shamdasani, P. N. (1990). *Focus Groups: Theory and practice* (Vol. 20). Newbury Park: SAGE Publications.

Strauss, A., & Corbin, J. (1998). *Basics of qualitative research: Techniques and procedures for developing grounded theory.* Thousand Oaks, California: Sage Publications.

Strehle, E. L., Whatley, A., Kurz, K. A., & Hausfather, S. J. (2001). Narratives of collaboration: Inquiring into technology integration in teacher education. *Journal of Technology and Teacher Education, 10*(1), 27-47.

Stuckey, B. (2004). *Making the most of the good advice: Meta-analysis of guidelines for establishing an internet-mediated community of practice.* Unpublished manuscript.

Teasley, S. D., & Roschelle, J. (1993). Constructing a joint problem space: The computer as a tool for sharing knowledge. In S. P. Lajoie & S. J. Derry (Eds.), *Computers as cognitive tools* (pp. 229-260). Hillsdale, New Jersey: Lawrence Erlbaum Associates.

Terehoff, I. (2002). Elements of adult learning in teacher professional development. *National Association of Secondary School Principals Bulletin, 86*(632), 65-77.

Tesch, R. (1990). *Qualitative research: Analysis types and software tools.* New York: The Falmer Press.

Thomas, G., Wineburg, S., Grossman, P., Myhre, O., & Woolworth, S. (1998). In the company of colleagues: An interim report on the development of a community of teacher learners.

Teaching and Teacher Education, 14(1), 21-32.

Thomas, M. (1999). Impacting on communication and learning: When communication technologies constrain communication. Retrieved 17th December, 2004, from http://www.aare.edu.au/99pap/tho99508.htm

Thorndike, E. (1928). The principles of teaching: Based on psychology. New York: A.G. Seiler.

Thrupp, R., & Hunt, J. (2005). Perceptions of Online Discussions by pre-service teachers: Unpublished Report, Central Queensland University.

Videbeck, R. (1973). Self-conception and the reactions of others. In M. Argyle (Ed.), Social Encounters: Readings in social interaction (pp. 331-339). Chicago: Aldine Publishing Company.

Vrasidas, C., & Zembylas, M. (2004). Online professional development: lessons from the field. Education and Training, 46(6/7), 326-334.

Waggoner, M. (1992). A case study approach to evaluation of computer conferencing. In A. R. Kaye (Ed.), Collaborative learning through computer conferencing: The Najaden papers (pp. 137-146). New York: Springer.

Warisse Turner, J., Grube, J. A., & Meyers, J. (2001). Developing an optimal match within online communities: An exploration of CMC support communities and traditional support. Journal of Communication, June 2001, 231-251.

Watts, G. D., & Castle, S. (1992). Electronic networking and the construction of professional knowledge. Phi Delta Kappan, 73, 684-689.

Webb, I., Robertson, M., & Fluck, A. (2004, December 2004). ICT, Professional Learning: Towards Communities of Practice. Paper presented at the AARE2004, Melbourne.

Wenger, E. (1998). *Communities of Practice: Learning as a social system*. Retrieved 9th November, 2004, from http://www.co-i-l.com/coil/knowledge-garden/cop/lss.shtml

White, C. (2003). *Language learning in distance education*. Cambridge: Cambridge University Press.

Wild, M. (1999). The anatomy of practice in the use of mailing lists: A case study. *Australian Journal of Educational Technology, 15*(2), 117-135.

Williams, F., Rice, R. E., & Rogers, E. M. (1988). *Research Methods and the New Media*. New York: The Free Press.

Williams, M. (1997). *Professional associations - supporting teacher communities*. Retrieved 9th November, 2004, from http://www.teachers.ash.org.au/williams/writing97/cinNZ.html

Wineburg, S., & Grossman, P. (1998). Creating a community of learners among high school teachers. *Phi Delta Kappan, 79*, 350-353.

Winitzky, N., & Kauchak, D. (1997). Constructivism in teacher education: Applying cognitive theory to teacher learning. In V. Richardson (Ed.), *Constructivist teacher education: Building new understandings* (pp. 59-83). London: The Falmer Press.

Woodruff, E. (1999). *Concerning the cohesive nature of CSCL Communities.* Paper presented at the Proceedings of Computer Supported Collaborative Learning '99 Conference, Mahwah, NJ.

Yin, R. K. (1994). *Case study research: Design and methods*. Thousand Oaks, CA: Sage.

Yin, R. K. (2003). *Applications of case study research* (Vol. 34). Newbury Park: SAGE Publications.

Zafeiriou, G., Nunes, J. M. B., & Ford, N. (2001). Using students' perceptions of participation in collaborative learning activities in the design of online learning environments. *Education for information, 19*, 83-106.

Zahner, J. (2002). Teachers explore knowledge management and e-learning as models for professional development. *TechTrends, 46*(3), 11-16.

Zhang, Y. (1999). Using the Internet for survey research: a case study. *Journal of the American Society for Information Science, 51*(1), 57-68.

Zibit, M. (2004). The peaks and valleys of online professional development. *eLearn Magazine, March 2004*(3), 3-16.

Zucker, D. M. (2001). Using case study methodology in nursing research. *The Qualitative Report, 6*(2).